BIBLE
PROPHECY
TRUE AND FALSE?

Dennis H. Helton

DEDICATION

This work is dedicated to my faithful wife, Christine, of 60 years.

Dennis D. Helton
2022

TABLE OF CONTENTS

SOME OF THE TOPICS COVERED

◆ What are the **Benefits of Bible Prophecy**?

◆ What is **The First and Greatest Prophecy**?

◆ What is **The Spirit of Prophecy**?

◆ What are **Relevant Prophecies of Latter Days**?

◆ Does prophecy prove that **Christ is the Messiah**?

◆ How can we recognize **False Prophets?**

◆ What is the meaning of **The End of the World**?

◆ Will the **Earth Literally Burn Up**?

◆ Who are **The Two Beasts of Revelation 13**?

◆ Why is Prophecy Sometimes Hard to Interpret?

◆ Is **Israel's Final National Restoration** Prophesied?

◆ Who is **the Rock of Salvation**?

◆ Are today's **Divine Healers** genuine?

INTRODUCTION

PROPHECY DEFINED

The Greek word for **prophecy** (Strong's # 4394, "propheteia," prop-ay-ti'-ah) means,

"To tell before." Some like to say that it is history written in advance. Bible schools use the word *eschatology* in reference *to prophecy*. Eschatology is the division of systematic theology dealing with the doctrine of *last things* such as Death, Resurrection, The Second Coming of Christ, end of the World (completion of the Age), Divine Judgment, and The Future State. A large part of the Bible is **prophecy**.

There are over 300 prophecies in the Old Testament that were fulfilled in the New Testament concerning Christ's "First Coming" (Viz, birth; life; betrayal; crucifixion; death; resurrection; ascension; et al). Much of the Bible was prophecy when it was written. Many Bible commentators believe that there are more prophecies yet to be fulfilled than have been fulfilled.

The Final Prophecy

It must be acknowledged that the final prophecy for all time is the "Apocalypse," or The Book of Revelation (The word Revelation means the "unveiling" or "revealing"). While exiled on the Isle of Patmos, the Lord Jesus told John the apostle how the age would end. Most of the Book of Revelation (chapters 6-19) concerns the 7-year Tribulation Period. The 7-Year Tribulation Period is also the same as "Daniel's 70th Week of Prophecy" - Daniel 9:27; the "Day of God's Vengeance" - Isaiah 61:2; 63:4; Jeremiah 46:10; the "Time of Jacob's Trouble" - Jeremiah 30:7. This Tribulation period is the final judgment of Israel and the purging of Jewish national unbelief. It is also a time when Gentile nations shall be judged along with unrepentant sinners (refer to the Olivet discourse of Matthew 24). Again, a remnant of Israel shall also be purged of her unbelief of rejecting Jesus, their promised Messiah, The last half (3 ½ years) of the

Tribulation Period is called "The Great Tribulation" because of the indescribable, horrendous judgments that will be poured out upon the earth. Some Bible teachers appropriately describe this period upon earth as the closest thing to Hell without being there.

There are those preachers (?) and liberal religionists who claim that we should not study the Book of Revelation seriously. They say, "because of the many signs and symbols, we are unable to understand." This writer completely disagrees with such a ludicrous and foolish statement. God would not waste His time, nor that of believers, by giving us a divinely inspired and preserved book that we could not understand ...though not fully, but in part at least. The book of Revelation is the culmination of earth's history.

The writer does not feel the urgency, but if time permits and God allows, the writer desires to write a commentary on the Book of Revelation; however; there are already good commentaries out there (Vi z: Lehman Strauss; James Knox; Oliver B. Greene; H. M. Freligh; Dr. J. Royce Thomason; et al). Note: The writer does not suppose he could add any better insight on prophecy.

Motives for Prophecy

Motives for Prophecy: Generally, there are two main reasons why people read prophecy. The non-serious readers love to read about future prophetical events purely out of curiosity, entertainment, and excitement (and that is not necessarily all wrong). They are drawn to the sensationalism of cataclysmic events coming upon the earth (great earthquakes; floods; giant hailstones from space; horrific storms; the moon turned as blood) and the identity of the Antichrist. There is much fascination about the identity of the beast out of the sea (Antichrist) of Revelation chapter 13 and his religious head-minister, the beast (false prophet) out of the earth. The beast out of the earth will rule co-regent for a time with Antichrist and then be destroyed by his political boss, the Antichrist (Revelation 18). The beast and the False Prophet are mentioned together in the book of Revelation

(Revelation 13:11-13; 16:13; 19:20; 20:10). Antichrist will foster demonic controlled armies during The Great Tribulation period. Nearly all religious people (saved or unsaved) are interested in the identity of the political and religious duo of Revelation.

The Antichrist (political ruler/antichrist government) is the beast out of the sea (nations; people; Mediterranean Sea). The false prophet (world religious ruler) along with his apostles of Hell, is the beast out of the earth. Both of these beasts persons are controlled by Satan.

The gospel of Christ is the good news, and the future good news is, "the Church (Body of Christ) is not appointed unto the wrath of the tribulation period" - (Romans 5:9; Revelation 3:10; 4:1; I Thessalonians 5:9, 10; Titus 2:13; I Thessalonians 4:13-18; I Corinthians 15:51-58).

[Note: Gospel = n. [S.godspell]; God, good, and spell, history, relation, narration, word, speech, that which is uttered, announced, sent or communicated; answering to a good or joyful message - "American Dictionary Of The English Language – Noah Webster 1828."] In other words, gospel is defined as God's Word, God's message, or God's news, not technically good news; of course the gospel is good news.]

Many believe that the antichrist person is living today (and he probably is). Even if antichrist is living today, his identity will not be publicly revealed in present times but will become known to the world during the time of the Tribulation Period.

Again, this period of time is Daniel's 70th Week of Prophecy (Daniel 9:27; 2 Thessalonians 2:3), the Time of Jacob's Trouble (Jeremiah 30:7), and a time of trouble such as never was since there was a nation (Daniel 12:1).. In other Scriptures (Isaiah), it is called the day of God's vengeance, the day of wrath, and the day of the LORD.

The un-paralleled, cascading world events during the Tribulation Period (Mark of the beast; Antichrist's order to kill all of the Jews) leave little doubt as to the identity of this 5th Gentile

World Emperor (Antichrist). Again, this evil world tyrant may be alive today (2 Thessalonians 2:3). It also appears that Roman Catholic scholars may have identified one of their own popes, Francis, as the final pope and the false prophet of the book of Revelation (this time, the writer agrees with religious, erroneous Rome. (Note: this writer speculates that there may be a forerunner of Antichrist alive today in imitation of God's program of John the Baptist; the Bible does not directly teach such a scenario). Perhaps Antichrist will be introduced to the world by the wonders performed by the false prophet as described in Revelation 13:11-15.

The serious student of prophecy is more concerned about The Signs of the Times and how they relate to governmental oppression/suppression upon civil freedoms and the freedom of preaching the Gospel. The serious students of Scriptures are also concerned with salvation and winning the lost to Christ before it is too late.

The student of prophecy is not greatly surprised at the Israeli-Palestinian great controversy and the attitude of the world concerning the Arab/Israeli conflict. The students of prophecy know that Israel is God's earthly timepiece for prophecy.

If the reader is not a serious student of prophecy, this writing may not appeal to him.

The Reason for the Title of This Writing

The writer titles this paper "Bible Prophecy" to distinguish it from the many false prophecies of contemporary times that are promoted under the pretense of "God's anointing." Of course, Satan mimics God's preachers with his own apostles of darkness (Matthew 7:15; I Timothy 4:1-2; 2 Timothy 4:3-4; 2 Peter 2:1, 18, 22; 2 Corinthians 11:13-15). Some latter-day false prophecies will be noted later in this writing.

Why Study Prophecy?

- **Prophecy** is exciting, especially to the Bible student and those who look for "the blessed hope and the glorious appearing of the great God and our Saviour Jesus Christ" (Titus 2:13; Philippians 3:20).

- Israel is **the key to prophecy** (Daniel 9:24-27). Gentile history is ancillary (subordinate; serves as an aid) to Jewish prophecy.

- **Prophecy** informs us of future events so that we might not remain ignorant of God's Plan of the Ages. "For I would not have you to be ignorant, brethren" I Thessalonians 4:13). Prophecy is the **key** that unlocks the future...making world events relevant to us.

- **Prophecy** (Scriptures) is needful for spiritual maturity (II Timothy 3:16-17).

- Scripture is called **Prophecy** "...as men were moved by the Holy Ghost" (2 Peter 1:21). The Scriptures are called prophecy because they are the divinely inspired Word of God, whether or not they contain future predictions.

- Fulfilled **prophecies** prove the divine origin of the Bible.

- Numerous fulfilled **prophecies concerning Christ's "First Coming" prove His deity.**

- **"...For the testimony of Jesus is the spirit of prophecy"** (Revelation 19:10; I Peter 1:11).

The Book of Revelation

The Book of Revelation, which is nearly all future prophecy, is called "prophecy."

Seven Times (Revelation 1:3; 11:6; 19:10; 22:7, 10, 18, 19). "Seven" is the number that signifies completion and the consummation of a matter (such as God's program of Seven Thousand Years culminating with Jesus on the throne of David). There are many "sevens" in the Book of Revelation that signify finality and completion. No, Mr. Mystic, God is not giving you a revelation that is extra-biblical (not included in the Bible). God's revelations come to us through **His Word**, not from dreams and visions. We have a more sure Word of prophecy (2 Peter 1:19;

Revelation 1:3; 22:7; Hebrews 1:1, 2). The Scriptures are sealed up in the final book of the Bible, the Book of Revelation. God is not presently giving extra-biblical revelations to a select few.

(Note: the writer is not discounting the possibility of God communicating by dreams or visions with those who may or may not have the Word of God.)

Again, if not for the Word of God and it's **prophecy**, how would we know about the Resurrection, The Second Coming of Christ, The Judgment Seat of Christ, The apostate harlot church, Antichrist, The Great Tribulation Period, The Kingdom Age, The Great White Throne Judgment, The Eternal State, New Jerusalem, etc.? If not for **prophecy**, we would be in darkness about much of the future: but God's children are children of light (Luke 16:8; John 12:36; Ephesians 5:8).

Dr. Graham Scroggie said, "Prophecy and miracles constitute the two great defenses of the Christian religion. Prophecy gives proof of the supernatural in WORDS. Miracles give proof of it in WORKS."

This paper is titled "Bible Prophecy" because there are no living prophets today receiving direct extra-biblical revelation from God (foretelling future events). The true predictive nature of prophetical future events must rely upon illumination and enlightenment by the **Holy Spirit** in accordance to the revealed prophecies in the Scriptures. God now speaks to us through **His Son, the Written Word** (Hebrews 1:1-2; John 1:1).

CHAPTER 1

RULES OF GENUINE PROPHECY

1.) Prophecy known prior to fulfillment

2.) Prophecy be beyond human foresight

3.) Prophecy details

4.) Sufficient time-lapse to exclude the prophet (or any other party) from fulfilling

5.) Clear and detailed fulfillment of prophecy

(**NOTE:** The gift of prophecy, whereby divine revelation is directly given by God to His prophets, shall fail [cease] when that which is perfect [completed canon of the pure Word of God] is come – I Corinthians 13:8-10; Psalms 12:6. **Man now receives illumination of Scriptures by the Holy Spirit** [John 17:7-13; I Corinthians 2:13-14], **not extra-biblical revelation**. Again, revelation of Scriptures ceased with John's book of Revelation.)

"So-called" Sacred Writings

Although all other "so-called" sacred writings such as the Book of Mormon, the Koran, the Vedas, the Dharma, and the Apocrypha (not the *Apocalypse* of Revelation 1:1), may contain plausible teachings, they are only of men. These "other" books are **not** inspired of God though they may contain factual material. Writings claiming divine inspiration are the same as substituting for the Word of God (Viz., Book of Mormon; Koran; Apocalypse; Adventists; et al).

Some New Age Bibles such as translations and paraphrases ("dynamic equivalences") from the Westcott-Hort/Nestle-Aland Greek manuscripts even "add to," and "take away" from the Word of God which is expressly forbidden (Revelation 22:18; Deuteronomy 4:2).

Genuine Christians do not corrupt the Word of God as do writers and editors of New Age Bibles (Viz., NIV; RSV; ASV;

NASV; ERV; New World Translation; New Jerusalem; NIV gender neutral; et al).

II Corinthians 2:17: For we are not **as many, which corrupt the word of God**: but as of sincerity, but as of God, in the sight of God speak we in Christ.

However, if any person does not believe Moses and the prophets (Scriptures), neither will they be persuaded though one rose from the dead (Luke 16:31; John 5:46).

The Preserved English Bible

God has **preserved** His Word(s) in the manuscripts of the OT Ben Chayyim Masoretic Hebrew and the NT Textus Receptus (Majority Text; Received Test; Byzantine Greek; Beza's 5th Edition of 1598). For English speaking people, the 1611 King James Bible is translated from the preserved manuscripts and is a trustworthy translation. We do not have the original autographs (manuscripts), but we do have apographs (copies of copies) that God preserved and protected.

In our present age, most New Age Bibles are translations or paraphrases (dynamic equivalences) from the corrupted line of the NT Greek texts. This Greek line of texts are of the Alexandrian/Siniaticus/Vaticanus/Westcott-Hort/Nestle-Aland stream and the OT text is of Ben Asher Hebrew manuscripts. It is sad to see that most denominations and sects are using the New Age Bibles that are products from corrupt manuscript sources. It is shameful that many pastors have spearheaded the usage of New Age Bibles and especially so without even having investigated their source.

See the writer's booklet, "NIV vs. KJV."

The Nature of Bible Prophecy

Bible prophecy is ambivalent ("near" and "far") in its "foretelling" aspect:

a) The prophecy, many times, has **a near or immediate fulfilling** (representation; counterpart). We commonly use "figure" or "type," (Hebrews 9:24; I Peter 3:21).

b) The **ultimate fulfilling** of the prophecy (perfect image or antitype) itself at **a distant future time** (Joel 2:28-32 cf. Acts 2:16).

Bible Prophecy is Also Ambivalent in its "Forth-telling" Aspect:

a) **Literal** application (Ezekiel 16)

b) **Spiritual** application (Ezekiel 16; Psalms 1:1-3...as to teaching spiritual truth even in parables (Matthew 13:45-51)

Bible prophecy may be divided into three divisions:

a) **Past:** fulfilled prophecy (as Christ's birth, life, death, resurrection)

b) **Present:** fulfilling prophecy (Christ's church being built; Jews regathered from the nations; moral character of the times; apostate religion; etc.)

c) **Future:** unfulfilled (but as certain as prophecy already fulfilled)

d) We have an example of the three divisions of prophecy in the book of Revelation, which is the capstone of all prophecy (Revelation 1:19).

   Revelation 1:19 *Write the things which thou hast seen, and the things which are, and the things which shall be hereafter;*

Bible Prophecy is Two-fold in Nature:

a) **Descriptive:** Forth-telling (spiritual insight) of things that have already happened (Acts 2:22-36).

b) **Predictive:** Foretelling (spiritual foresight) of things that are going to happen according to "written" Scriptures (2 Peter 3:10-13).

2 Peter 3:10 But the day of the Lord will come as a thief in the night; in the which the heavens shall pass away with a great noise, and the elements shall melt with fervent heat, the earth also and the works that are therein shall be burned up. 11 Seeing then that all these things shall be dissolved, what manner of persons ought ye to be in all holy conversation and godliness, 12 Looking for and hasting unto the coming of the day of God, wherein the heavens being on fire shall be dissolved, and the elements shall melt with fervent heat? 13 Nevertheless we, according to his promise, look for new heavens and a new earth, wherein dwelleth righteousness.

The Major Prophets

The Major Prophets: (not major because they are of greater importance but mainly because of their length). Jeremiah has more words than Isaiah but less chapters.

Most prophecy is centered about Messiah and Israel: however, Gentiles are also spoken about.

* Isaiah's Prophecy: Messiah and Israel

* Jeremiah's Prophecy: Israel's captivity and return to their land

* Ezekiel's Prophecy: Israel's return to their own land and the Millennial Temple

* Daniel's Prophecy: 490 years of the times of the Jewish people and Gentiles and their final antichrist leader

* Zechariah's Prophecy: Second Coming events…

  • Antichrist; idol shepherd (Zechariah 11:15-17)

  • Armageddon (Zechariah 14:1-3)

- Israel's conversion (Zechariah 14:4-11)

- Long life in Jerusalem (Zechariah 8:3-8)

- Feast of Tabernacles (Zechariah 14:16-21)

- The Kingship of Christ is emphasized in all Major Prophets and 9 of the Minor Prophets.

CHAPTER 2

WHY IS PROPHECY HARD TO SORT OUT?

Why Aren't the Scriptures More Explicit on Prophecy?

ANSWER: A certain degree of obscurity and veiling is necessary in prophecy, especially to the eye of the unbeliever (Matthew 13:11). If prophecy were to be too definitive, it might intrude into man's free will of every day affairs in life. Men would abuse and twist prophecies for other purposes and goals, instead of truth. Also, if the prophecies were spelled out too clearly, the skeptics could claim that that was the very cause of the prophecy's fulfillment. In other words, unbelievers could say that believers accomplished the fulfillment of the prophecy in order to make the prediction true.

<u>For example, upon the direction of an angel of the Lord in a dream, Joseph, the foster-father of Jesus did fulfill a prophecy:</u>

Matthew 2:23: And he (Joseph) came and dwelt in a city called Nazareth: that it might be fulfilled which was spoken by the prophets, He shall be called a Nazarene.

With the scattered and sometimes illogical order that prophecy is veiled within (with figures, types, customs, parables, etc.), a diligent study and comparison of Scriptures is required. Of course, the Holy Spirit leads and guides His saints in all truth (John 16:13).

Prophecy is Literal

Prophecy is Literal Although prophecy is literal, that does not rule out symbolism, figures, speech idioms, customary usage of Bible language, rhetoric, customary rules of grammar, national culture, satire, etc.

Literal data is included in prophecy, such as: NAMES (Isaiah 45:1-3); PLACES (Micah 5:2); CHRONOLOGY (Daniel 7); DETAILS (Psalms 22; Isaiah 53; Luke 19:41-44); TIMES (Daniel 9:24-27; Jeremiah 25:11-12).

Bible prophets did not prophesy for money or gain and were often persecuted and impoverished. How unlike many present day "prosperity" preachers!

Four (4) Major Aspects of the Supernatural Element of Prophecy

Inspiration

1) Inspiration: In the original Scriptures (initial autographs), the exact **Words of God** were imparted by the Holy Spirit. Peter says,

"**...**holy men of God spake as they were moved by the Holy Ghost"- (2 Peter 1:21).

These **inspired Words** (2 Timothy 3:16) are totally different from poets, writers, and speakers.

> **2 Timothy 3:16** All scripture is given by inspiration of God, and is profitable for doctrine, for reproof, for correction, for instruction in righteousness:

Actually, **every Word** that proceeds out of the mouth of God is **God-breathed** (Matthew 4:4; Luke 4:4). Declarations such as, "Thus saith the Lord," and The Lord spake saying," appear over 2,000 times in the OT.)

> **Matthew 4:4** But he answered and said, It is written, Man shall not live by bread alone, but by every word that proceedeth out of the mouth of God.

Preservation

2) Preservation: The Word of God has been miraculously and wonderfully preserved (Psalms 12:6-7; 119:89; Isaiah 40:8; Matthew 24:35; I Peter 1:23-25).

> ***1 Peter 1:23*** *Being born again, not of corruptible seed, but of incorruptible, by the word of God, which liveth and abideth for ever.* ***24*** *For all flesh is as grass, and all the glory of man as the flower of grass. The grass withereth, and the flower thereof falleth away:* ***25*** *But the word of the Lord endureth for ever. And this is the word which by the gospel is preached unto you.*

Also see Psalms 78:1-8; 105:8; 119:111, 152, 160; Proverbs 22:20-21; Ecclesiastes 3:13; Isaiah 30:8; 59:21; Matthew 4:4; John 12:49-50; 17:8; I Peter 1:23.

If the original autographs have not been preserved in accurat copies of copies (apographs), who could know what the originals are? **No one has the originals!** Even if the originals were available, not everyone could have access to the single canon of originals. There must be preserved inerrant copies of copies to facilitate the reading by billions. We trust God.

Revelation

3) Revelation: The *unveiling* and *revealing* to men things that they otherwise could never know. This revelation directly to man ceased with the Book of Revelation. No one today is receiving direct prophecies from God (though some claim private revelations).

Sometimes, NT writers paraphrased OT writers. Compare Amos 9:11 to Acts 15:16. Compare Isaiah 53:1-12 to I Peter 1:11. You can be sure the meaning is the same even if phrased differently.

Illumination

4) Illumination: This is the Work of the Holy Spirit in enlightening the New Testament saint's spiritual understanding of Scriptures (John 16:12-15; I Corinthians 2:11-14).

It may shock some to know that **not all men** of the OT who prophesied were good or obedient men. Examples:

1. Balaam: (Numbers 22:38; 23:26)

2. King Saul: (I Samuel 10:10-12; 19:20-24)

3. Prophet of Bethel: (I Kings 13:7-10; 20:22; 26)

4. Caiaphas: (John 11:49-52)

False Prophets

Jesus, the Master Prophet, warned us about false prophets (Matthew 7:15; Mark 13:22); so did Peter (2 Peter 2:1) and John (I John 4:1). Paul tells us that Satan's ministers are transformed as ministers of righteousness ((2 Corinthians 11:15). These copy-cat ministers of Satan easily deceive nominal religious people.

CHAPTER 3

THE GREATEST MODERN-DAY PROPHECY: ISRAEL

Israel as a nation is the greatest modern-day prophecy. The Jews were without a kingdom or a country for 2,500 years. They had been dispersed to nations all over the earth, but they remained a distinct people. So after about 2,500 years, they became a nation on **May 14, 1948**. One writer says, "Jews came from 120 nations and speaking 83 different languages." Thousands of Jews are irresistibly drawn to Israel annually.

During World War II, God enabled a Jewish chemist, Dr. Chaim Weizmann, to discover a way to make acetone (out of maize/corn) which was essential to the manufacture of gun powder and explosives. This was vital to the British in winning the war. Britain, under the Balfour Declaration, awarded the Jews a Palestinian homeland in May 1948 (Previously, Britain had opposed the Jews). Immediately afterwards. **(1948)**, Arab armies from five nations (representing 80 million people) attacked tiny Israel with its small army of 19,000 soldiers who were trying to defend on five fronts. After a seeming defeat, Israel threw the enemy back and smashed their combined military power. The United Nations stepped in to rescue Israel's enemy.

In **1956**, Israel forced Egypt to reopen the Suez Canal, ensuring the continuation of world trade.

On June 4, **1967**, Cairo radio predicted, "We will wipe Israel off the face of the map, and no Jew will remain alive." On June 5, the Arabs attacked with 650,000 men, 2,700 tank, and 1,090 aircraft. Israel had 300,000 men, 800 tanks, and 400 planes. In six days, the Israelis smashed the attacking armies. Israel then occupied the city of Old Jerusalem.

In **1974**, the Arabs launched a surprise attack on Israel on Yom Kippur (Day of Atonement), the holiest day of the year. The battle was stopped by an American-Soviet arranged cease-fire after a near Middle East nuclear war.

Israel was preserved as the Scriptures prophesied 2,500 years ago (Isaiah 62:1-4; 66:8-9; Ezekiel 37:21). God promised to keep them and revive them in the last days. All prophecy revolves around Jesus and His chosen national people. Israel is God's earthly time-piece.

Israel in Prophecy

Israel in prophecy: (*Message of the Christian Jew,* May-June 2000, p. 2)

1. **Prophecy:** Israel would be regathered from all the countries where they had been scattered - (Ezekiel 36:24; Isaiah 49:12)

   Fulfillment: After 50 years as a restored nation (May 14-15, 1948), Israel has a Jewish population near five million (at the time of this writing).

2. **Prophecy:** Jews would rebuild the ancient cities and reclaim the land - (Ezekiel 36:9-10, 33-35)

   Fulfillment: Since 1948, Israel has been systematically rebuilding her ancient cities and also has become one of the largest exporters of agricultural goods and citrus fruits in the Middle East.

3. **Prophecy:** Israel would be partitioned by the nations of the world - (Joel 3:2)

   Fulfillment: On November 29, 1947, the United Nations General Assembly approved a motion to partition Palestine into two separate states.

4. **Prophecy:** Israel would be voted into existence by the nations of the world - (Ezekiel 38:8)

   Fulfillment: On May 16, 1949, Israel was accepted as a member nation of the United Nations.

5. **Prophecy:** Israel would regain her land through warfare - (Ezekiel 38:8)

Fulfillment: Four major wars have been fought in the Middle East since 1948. Israel has successfully defended her territory each time, even against overwhelming odds.

6. **Prophecy:** Once Israel returned to her land, she would not be removed from it - (Amos 9:15)

Fulfillment: Attempts by the Palestine Liberation Organization to remove Israel from her land have failed miserably.

The Jews were God's **peculiar treasure** in the Old Testament (Psalms 135:4; Exodus 19:5). Israel is the **apple** (pupil) **of God's eye** (Deuteronomy 32:10; Psalms 17:8; Zachariah 2:8). Israel is the **treasure hid in a field** (Exodus 19:5; Deuteronomy 14:2; Psalms 135:4; Matthew 13:44). Israel is God's **indestructible national people**.

In Israel, there is much talk about resuming Old Testament sacrifices. A "Red Heifer" was born on a Jewish farm. This was the first in 2,000 years. This Red Heifer was needed for the Jewish ordinance of **The Law for Water of Separation**, which was for purification for sin (Numbers 19:2, 9, 21). A group of Jews, headed up by Gershon Salomon is making plans to build the Temple foundation where or near the Islamic Dome of the Rock is now located. Scholars say that this is also the site of Solomon's Temple (Some disagree and say that this is not the exact location of the Jewish Temple site). Last reports say that the materials needed for this project are already gathered and waiting for the go-ahead to build. We know that the next Temple will be used by Antichrist and his false prophet to declare that the entire world should worship the Antichrist, the man of sin. See 2 Thessalonians 2:3, 8-9; Revelation 13:1, 11, 15.

Born in a Day

While many of the Jews have been re-gathered as a national people, there are still far more Jews in America and Russia than in Israel. The Jewish nation has not received spiritual life as yet. Collectively, the Jews are in a state of unbelief and spiritually dead concerning Jesus their Messiah. In a very brief time in the near future, spiritual Israel will be "born in a day" and will acknowledge Jesus Christ as their Messiah (Isaiah 66:8; Zechariah 13:6). This will be the spiritual restoration of Israel.

CHAPTER 4

THE SUFFERING MESSIAH

The Suffering Messiah (Genesis 3:15; Isaiah 53; 55; Psalm 22) is the Greatest Prophecy in the OT and it is in Reference to the Redemption of Man (I Timothy 3:16; Galatians 4:4)

What person is there in the whole world that ever lived could answer to the 53rd chapter of Isaiah other than Jesus Christ? This Scripture alone should convince any unbelieving Jew or Gentile that Jesus is the promised Messiah.

Isaiah 53:3-6: He (*Jesus*) is despised and rejected of men; a Man of sorrows, and acquainted with grief: and we (Jews and Gentiles) hid as it were our faces from Him (Jesus); He (Jesus) was despised, and we esteemed Him (Jesus) not. Surely He (Jesus) hath borne our griefs, and carried our sorrows: yet we did esteem Him (Jesus) stricken, smitten of God, and afflicted. But He (Jesus) was wounded for our transgressions, He (Jesus) was bruised for our iniquities: the chastisement of our peace was upon Him (Jesus); and with His (Jesus) stripes we are healed. All we like sheep have gone astray; we have turned every one to his own way; and the LORD hath laid on Him (Jesus) the iniquity of us all.

Sadly, unbelieving rabbis ignore this Scripture concerning their Messiah. There is Only One True God. All others are dunghill deities of no value

> Isaiah 44:6: "Thus saith **the LORD** (YHWH; Jehovah; God the Father) *the King of Israel, and* **His Redeemer** (Jesus; God the Son) *the Lord of hosts; I am the first, and I am the last; and beside Me there is no God."*

These two persons of the Trinity are saying in unison, *"...beside Me there is no God."* Both the Father, as King of

Israel, and the Son, as the Redeemer of men, speak here as ONE and declare both their unity and deity.

> *Revelation 22:13: "I am Alpha and Omega, the beginning and the end, the first and the last."*

This is the glorified Christ speaking in Revelation 22:13.

The Two Comings of Christ

The two comings of Christ to earth are usually referred to as, "The First and Second Advents of Christ."

First Advent

Jesus came the first time to seek and save the lost.

> **Luke 19:10** *For the Son of man is come to seek and to save that which was lost.*

This was possible because Jesus died as the sacrificial Lamb of God for sinful man. God's holiness demanded a perfect sacrifice and Jesus was the only one willing, worthy, and able to pay the supreme price necessary for the forgiveness for sin. Jesus Was and Is God's Only Begotten Son who Himself was God manifested in the flesh. Jesus made the way of salvation possible between a Holy God and sinful man. Jesus did all of the work for salvation and man only has to believe (repentance being inherent of true faith). Man must trust in the mercy of God's provision for sin (Luke 13:3; John 3:16; Ephesians 2:8, 9; Romans 10:9-10, 13; Matthew 11:28). Jesus died as a substitute for all sinners (I Timothy 2:4, 6; 4:10; 2 Peter 3:9; John 3:16), whosoever is willing to receive Him (John 1:12).

> *Philippians 2:6-8: Who, being in the form of God, thought it not robbery to be equal with God: But made Himself of no reputation, and took upon Him the form of a servant, and **was made in the likeness of men**: And being found **in fashion as a man,** He humbled himself, and became obedient unto death, even the death of the cross.*

Cf. I Timothy 3:16; John 3:16; Galatians 2:20.

Second Advent

As certain as the First Advent of Christ, so is His future Second Advent. However, at His Second Advent, He does not come as a Lamb to the slaughter, but **He comes as King of Kings and Lord of Lords** in great and terrible judgment of the world and sinners. At His Second Coming, the cup of iniquity of the Gentile nations will be full and running over. The Gentile nations will be defeated and Israel will be purged of her sin of unbelief and the rejection of her Messiah.

> *Revelation 19:15-16: And out of His mouth goeth a sharp sword (Word of God), that with it He should smite the nations: and He shall rule them with a rod of iron: and He treadeth the winepress of the fierceness and wrath of Almighty God. And He hath on His vesture and on His thigh a name written,* ***KING OF KINGS, AND LORD OF LORDS****.*

This time of The Great Tribulation will be a time of horrendous judgments poured out upon earth. Even now, the sinner is only promised today; there is no promise of tomorrow.

> *2 Corinthians 6:2: (For He saith, I have heard thee in a time accepted, and in the day of salvation have I succoured thee: behold,* ***now*** *is the accepted time; behold,* ***now*** *is the day of salvation.)*

> *John 8:24: I said therefore unto you, that* ***ye shall die in your sins: for if ye believe not that I am He****, ye shall die in your sins.*

These words of Jesus were spoken to the religious, unbelieving Pharisees of Judaism, but the same message applies to all who reject the deity of Jesus. The sinner can plead the mercy of God today, but he is not promised tomorrow. While there is life, there is hope.

Sleep well tonight because if you are an unbeliever, it could be your last day upon earth! Remember, there is no limbo state, middle ground, purgatory, la la land, or place for a second chance for salvation after death. There are only two places for deceased persons upon death, Heaven or Hell. The choice is entirely up to the reader.

> *Luke 12:16-21: And He (Jesus) spake a parable unto them, saying, The ground of a certain rich man brought forth plentifully: And he thought within himself, saying, What shall I do, because I have no room where to bestow my fruits? And he said, This will I do: I will pull down my barns, and build greater; and there will I bestow all my fruits and my goods. And I will say to my soul, Soul, thou hast much goods laid up for many years; take thine ease, eat, drink and be merry; But God said unto him, Thou fool, **this night thy soul shall be required of thee**: then whose shall those things be, which thou hast provided?*

Is any worldly gain (which no person can keep) worth exchanging for the loss of his/her soul, which will exist forever in Hell?

Second Coming of Christ is in Two Stages

Actually, the Second Coming of Christ is in two stages. In the first stage, Jesus comes for His church to meet Him in the air (I Corinthians 15:51-58; I Thessalonians 4:13-18. In the second state, Jesus literally comes to earth with His saints that He had called up in the air seven years prior.

First the Rapture

First is Christ coming for the church which is the Resurrection (Rapture), followed by the Tribulation Period, and the Second Coming.

Between the First Resurrection (Translation; Rapture; Metamorphosis) and Christ's Second Coming to earth, there is a period of Seven Years Duration. This brief period of time is the final week of Daniel's Seventy Weeks of Prophecy (Daniel 9:27) and Jewish calendar time; called, *"The Time of Jacob's Trouble"* (Jeremiah 30:7).

> ***Jeremiah 30:7*** *Alas! for that day is great, so that none is like it: it is even the time of Jacob's trouble; but he shall be saved out of it.*

His Second Coming to Earth

Jerusalem shall be trodden down of the Gentiles, until the time of the Gentiles shall be fulfilled (Luke 21:24). The end of this 7-Year Period is the end of world Gentile rule. The description of this 7-Year period of judgment is described in Revelation, chapters 6-19. Before the beginning of the Tribulation Period, Christ comes **for** His Bride (the church), and catches them up in clouds to meet Him in the air (I Thessalonians 4:13-18; 5:8; Revelation 4:1; I Corinthians 15:51-58). Christ comes **with** His saints [Bride; Church] about seven years later at His Second Coming to earth (Jude 1:14).

> ***Jude 14*** *And Enoch also, the seventh from Adam, prophesied of these, saying, Behold, the Lord cometh with ten thousands of his saints*

> ***1 Thessalonians 4:13*** *But I would not have you to be ignorant, brethren, concerning them which are asleep, that ye sorrow not, even as others which have no hope.* ***14*** *For if we believe that Jesus died and rose again, even so them also which sleep in Jesus will God bring with him.* ***15*** *For this we say unto you by the word of the Lord, that we which are alive and remain unto the coming of the Lord shall not prevent them which are asleep.* ***16*** *For the Lord himself shall descend from heaven with a shout, with the voice of the archangel, and with the trump of God: and the dead in Christ shall rise first:* ***17*** *Then we which are alive and remain shall be caught up together with them in the clouds, to meet the Lord in the air: and so shall we ever be with the Lord.* ***18*** *Wherefore comfort one another with these words.*

The Bride of Christ (True Church)

The Bride of Christ (true Church) will be spared God's wrath (Romans 5:9; I Thessalonians 5:9; Titus 2:13; Revelation 3:10) during this time of great world judgments.

> ***1 Thessalonians 5:9*** *For God hath not appointed us to wrath, but to obtain salvation by our Lord Jesus Christ,*

Jesus will return with His Bride of ten thousands of saints, to earth (Jude 1:14) after the tribulation period of 7 years. Jesus raptures His Bride about seven years prior to His Second Coming to earth. Christ does not come to earth at the time of the First Resurrection (commonly referred to as the Rapture or Translation). Jesus calls the saved up to meet Him in the air. The Church is not appointed to the wrath of the Tribulation Period (Romans 5:9; Revelation 3:10; I Thessalonians 5:9; Titus 2:13).

Christ will bring His Church with Him when He returns to earth at His Second Coming (Jude 14; Revelation 19:14).

The Church does not remain upon earth during the 7-year Tribulation Period which is significantly Jewish time (Daniel 9:27; I Corinthians 15:51-58; Revelation 3:10; 4:1). Again, the Church is not appointed to the wrath of the Tribulation Period (Romans 5:9; Revelation 3:10; I Thessalonians 5:9; Titus 2:13).

A Harlot Religious System

There will be a harlot religious system (Bride of Antichrist- Revelation chapters 13, 17 and 18) upon earth both before and during the Tribulation Period (religion and state will merge). During the Tribulation Period, "Political" Babylon will destroy "Religious" Babylon (Revelation chapter 18).

7-Year Tribulation Period

This 7-Year Tribulation Period is primarily a time of the purging of Israel's unbelief and rejection of their Jewish Messiah. It also includes the judgments upon Gentile nations who have persecuted Israel (these goat nations shall be set to the left hand of Jesus, Matthew 25:32-33). Gentile world domination will cease and Israel will be the chief of the nations during the following Millennium. Again, this 7-Year Jewish time is called Daniel's 70th Week of Prophecy (Daniel 9:24-27) and The Time of Jacob's Trouble (Jeremiah 30:7).

The phony religion (synagogue of Satan) is called a woman with the writing of a name upon her forehead, MYSTERY BABYLON THE GREAT, THE MOTHER OF HARLOTS AND ABOMINATIONS OF THE EARTH (Revelation 17:4, 5). The evil head of this monstrous Jezebel religion will be the False Prophet (Revelation 13:11-15). This religious synagogue of Satan and house of devils will rule co-regent with Antichrist (Revelation 13:11-14; 16:13; 19:20; 20:10).

Israel's Regathering

God has not forgotten Israel. For Israel's regathering, see II Samuel 7:10-17; Psalms 135:4; Isaiah 11:11; Jeremiah 7:7; 31:31-33; Ezekiel 37; Hosea 6:1-3; Amos 9:15; Zephaniah 3:14-20; Zechariah 10:6-12; 14:1-4

Israel was God's elect national people called out from among the Gentile world in the Old Testament (Deuteronomy 7:6-8). Israel will be the principal nation determining major future events of the world. Actually, the Gentile nations shall be judged in accordance to their treatment of the oppressed people of the world and especially of Israel (Matthew 25:32-46; Revelation 16:16; Ezekiel 38:38). For its support of Israel, America is hated by many countries and especially the perennial enemies of Israel, the Islamic Palestinians and Muslim terrorists. Most of Israel's chief enemies are Ishmaelites (Ishmael's descendants) and Edomites (Esau's descendants).

Israel's Enemies

(**Note**: The Ishmaelites [descendants of Abraham's son, Ishmael] and Edomites [descendants of Isaac's son, Esau] were always opposed to Israel in the Old Testament. The Islamists erroneously claim that the blessing of God came to them through Abraham's son, Ishmael, not Isaac.)

In the future, the world political situation will greatly intensify in wars because of Israel. Though all the people of the earth be gathered together against Israel and burden themselves with it, they shall be cut in pieces. Even today, it appears that the whole world is garnered together against tiny Israel (Europe; Asia; Middle East; United Nations; etc). The bigoted and radical Islamic hate-mongers protest the right for Israel to even exist as a nation and are gradually gaining support from the nations of the world. Even America (under President Obama), which has been Israel's chief supporter, is pressuring Israel into shameless concessions to Islamic radicals, urging a "land for peace treaty." The world wants Israel to give up land to the radical Muslims for alleged peaceful co-existence with them.   While America traverses the globe to expunge terrorism, she has a blind eye to the murderous actions of rabid Palestinians hurling rockets constantly at Israel. The time is drawing near when the chief prince (*Rosh of Russia with her army chiefly of Muslim soldiers)* of Meshech (*Moscow of Russia*) and Tubal (*Tobolsk of Russia*) with her hordes, Persia (*modern Iran*), Libya and Ethiopia (*parts of Africa*); Gomer (*Germany*); Togarmah (*Turkey/Armenia*), and many people (*especially Islamists*) will come against Israel (Psalms 83; Ezekiel chapters 38-39).   God will personally dispose of the invaders (the interpretations of the identities of these nations are of the writer's opinion and should be noted).

The threat of nuclear war hovers about the Mid-East. It is rumored that Iran (*Persia*) is striving to develop nuclear capability and be sure that the fanatical Muslims will use the nuclear devices if they are able to get them (There are some who predict that Iran may buy nuclear bombs from North Korea). Islam's goal is to destroy Israel, even if they themselves (Islamists) have to suffer great losses.

In Ezekiel 38:12, we are told that Gog (*chief prince*) will go to Israel with the intent to take a spoil, and to take a prey. The writer knows that gold and silver have great value but doubts that this is the reason for the assault against Israel. "Oil" is the ruling commodity of today's world of industry and machinery. Could it be that large reserves of oil may be discovered in Israel in the latter days and that will be the reason for the Gog (chief *prince*) invasion of Israel? The World Energy Council estimates that massive reserves of shale oil are confirmed just 30 miles southwest of Jerusalem could eventually yield as many as 250 billion barrels of oil. The USA is thought to have 1.5 billion barrels of untapped shale oil in un-mined deposits in Colorado. There are verses in the Bible that appear to support the possibility of huge oil discoveries in Israel. The Scripture makes direct reference to "oil" inside Israel's boundaries (Deuteronomy 32:113; 33:24). We have Asher dipping his feet in oil. Asher was a tribe located in the NW part of Israel, and not close to Jerusalem where the shale oil deposits were discovered. In Exodus 32:24, we have the statement about Israel sucking "honey out of the rock" and "oil out of the flinty rock." Perhaps the "spoil and prey" is this great oil discovery in Israel and the reason Gog (Russia), Persia (Iran), Ethiopia, Libya, Gomer (Germany), and Togormah (Turkey) will invade. Without oil, the machineries of a country cannot function.

(Note: There is an unverified claim that technology has advanced to the stage that energy may be derived from sand grains that will replace energy sources of oil, gas and coal and at a much cheaper cost. The writer has doubts to this claim.)

Another popular reason touted for the invasion of Israel is the wealth of the Dead Sea (phosphates; bromides; minerals) which is estimated to be valued over a trillion dollars.

God is not finished with backsliding Israel and His watchful eye is upon them. Again, "He that touches Israel touches "the apple (pupil) of God's eye" (Deuteronomy 32:10; Psalms 17:8; Zechariah 2:8).

Reasons Why God Chose Israel

◆ To be God's witnesses to the Gentile nations (Isaiah 43:10; 44:8)

◆ To pen and preserve the Scriptures (Romans 3:1-2)

◆ To bring forth the Son of God (Romans 9:5)

◆ The Lord loved them (Deuteronomy 7:8)

◆ Sworn unto your Jewish fathers (Deuteronomy 7:8)

◆ God made an unconditional covenant with Abraham and confirmed it with Isaac, Jacob and their seed.

◆ To show forth His praises (Isaiah 43:21)

◆ To be His peculiar treasure (Psalms 135:4; Matthew 13:44)

◆ To be His covenant people (Exodus 34:10; Isaiah 61:8)

◆ To be a light for the Gentiles (Isaiah 42:6)

◆ To inherit the earth (Isaiah 49:8)

◆ For God's holy name's sake (Ezekiel 36:22-23)

Israel is Under God's Watchful Eye

He Gives a Warning Concerning Her

> *Genesis 12:3: And I will bless them that bless thee, and **curse him that curseth thee:** and in thee shall all families of the earth be blessed*

Abraham and His Offspring

There are those that think that the blessing and curse of Genesis 12:3 applies only to Abraham and not the nation of Israel. However, this applies to both Abraham and his offspring. The blessing is repeated to Isaac and Jacob. Nowhere else in Scriptures is a blessing and a curse applied to an individual person. Since Abraham is the progenitor of the nation of Israel (Genesis 12:7) and considering many other related Scriptures, the writer believes that the blessing and curse is in reference to Abraham's descendants (Genesis 27:29b). We find the same blessing and curse in reference to Israel in Numbers 24:2-9:

> *Numbers 24:9: He (Israel) couched down, he lay down as a lion, and as a great lion: who shall stir him up?* **Blessed is he that blesseth thee, and cursed is he that curseth thee.**

Abraham cannot be disassociated from Israel (Psalms 105:6, 9, 42, 43; Hebrews 6:13, 14), for Israel is the national seed of Abraham. God even told Abram that He would make Abram a great nation (Genesis 12:2).

Two of the Greatest Prophecies in Scriptures

Two of the Greatest Prophecies in Scriptures Concern the Two Comings of Christ

> *Genesis 3:15: And I will put enmity between thee and* **the woman**, *and between* **thy seed** *and* **her seed**; **It shall bruise thy head**, *and thou shalt* **bruise his heel**.

Interpretation of Genesis 3:15

- **The woman:** Israel (Revelation 12:1-6; Genesis 37:9)

- **Her seed:** Offspring; Christ (Revelation 12:1-6)

- **Thy (Satan's) seed:** Offspring; Primarily Satan's cohort, the antichrist (Revelation 13:4-8; 2 Thessalonians 2:3-9), but also his dummies (Genesis 4:8; Matthew 26:14-16; 27:3; Luke 22:3; John 13:27; 17:12).

- **Bruise His (Christ) heel:** a temporary wound to Christ (Psalms 22; Isaiah 53:5-6; Romans 5:8; Hebrews 2:9; 9:26)

- **Bruise thy (Satan) head:** a permanent wound to Satan (Revelation 19:20; 20:10)

Satan bruised the heel of Jesus at Calvary's cross (only by God's permission), but Jesus also bruised Satan at Calvary's cross (John 17:4; 19:30) and shall bruise his head permanently in the lake of fire at a future time (Revelation 20:10).

The Antichrist

The Antichrist is called "that man of sin, the son of perdition" (2 Thessalonians 2:3).

> ***2 Thessalonians 2:3*** *Let no man deceive you by any means: for that day shall not come, except there come a falling away first, and that man of sin be revealed, the son of perdition;*

It is interesting to note that only one other person in the Bible is referred to as the *"son of perdition,"* Judas Iscariot (John 17:12). Also, other than the devil himself, there is only one other individual in the Bible that is referred to as a devil (Greek "diabolos"), Judas Iscariot. Actually, many students of the Bible believe that Judas Iscariot will be the incarnated antichrist personage because of the Scriptures of John 17:12 and John 6:70.

> *John 6:70, 71: Jesus answered them, Have not I chosen you twelve, and one of you is a devil? He spake of Judas Iscariot the son of Simon: for he that should betray him, being one of the twelve.*

Of course, it must be observed that Jesus called Judas "a" (indefinite article) devil, not "the" (definite article) devil. Too, Jesus told the unbelieving Pharisees that they were of their father the devil (John 8:44) and we are told in I John 3:8 that "He that comitteth sin (a "life style" of sin) is of the devil."

Add to the list of the enemies of Israel and her God: Pharaoh, Antiochus Ephipanes, Haman, Herod, Hitler, Satan's ministers (2 Corinthians 11:13-15), and many other antichrist personages.

Christians (?) Opposed to Israel

In the past, many *professing* Christians have persecuted and opposed Jews but this is a rarity for *genuine* Christians.

Replacement Theology

Today, some Christians are opposed to the Jewish people because of Israel's national unbelief. Some Christians mistakenly suppose that God is finished with the nation of Israel. They erroneously suppose that God has replaced Israel with the Church (called **"Replacement Theology"**). Of course, this is totally untrue. Israel is God's elect national people and God always preserved a remnant of Israelite believers. God is married to her (Jeremiah 3:14).

Israel's New Covenant of Grace

Actually, Gentiles were admitted to God's grace and mercy through Israel's New Covenant of Grace (Jeremiah 31:31-34; Hebrews 7:22; 8:6). Some of the natural branches of the good olive tree (Israel) were broken off and cast away because of unbelief. We Gentiles, wild branches of a wild olive tree, were graffed (grafted) in the good olive tree, which was contrary to nature. Gentiles, as well as Jews, stand by faith (Romans 11:13-28).

Romans 11:18: Boast not against the branches. But if thou boast, thou bearest not the root, but the root thee.

CHAPTER 5

THE SECOND GREAT PROPHECY IN SCRIPTURES

The Second Coming of Christ for the Church

As stated before, as sure as Christ came the **first time** to seek and save the lost (Matthew 18:11), so will He come the **second time** to judge Israel (not the Bride of Christ, the Church) and the Gentile world (Acts 17:31; 2 Timothy 4:1; Jude 15; Revelation 19:11). Because of the erroneous teaching of "preterism" (preterists say that The Second Coming of Christ and other major prophecies have already been fulfilled), there are not many churches that preach on the **Second Coming of Christ** and the writer doubts that some who do teach it even believe it. Christ will literally descend to the earth and every eye shall see Him. After Jesus judges Israel and the Gentile nations of the world, He will rule the earth from the throne of David in Jerusalem for a thousand glorious years (Revelation chapter 20).

As has already been mentioned several times, before Christ comes to earth the second time, there is a Coming of Christ in the heavens above, in the air, to receive His bride, the Church, which is comprised of both saved Jews and Gentiles (Titus 2:13; I Corinthians 15:51-58; I Thessalonians 4:13-18; 5:9; Romans 5:9; Revelation 3:10; 4:1). In this meeting **in the air** (First Resurrection; Rapture), Christ comes "for" His Church. In Christ's Second Coming about seven years after The First Resurrection, He will return "with" His Church to earth (Jude 14-15; Revelation 19:14). Of course, this rapture (catching away of the Church), occurs between the First Coming of Christ to earth and His Second Coming to earth.

(**NOTE**: The First Resurrection of saints is likened unto a crop harvest which is made up of three parts,)

a. The Firstfruits of Christ's saints;

b. The Main Harvest of the Church,

c. and the Gleanings composed of the Tribulation saints (a post-Tribulation of saints).

The New Testament (NT) Church Was Not Revealed in the OT

Ephesians 3:5-6: **Which in other ages was not made known** *unto the sons of men, as it is* **now revealed** *unto his holy apostles and prophets by the Spirit; That the Gentiles should be fellow-heirs, and of the same body and partakes of his promise in Christ by the gospel.*

The building of the NT Church is prophecy being fulfilled before our very eyes. Of course, there are many imitations of the true church.

Matthew 16:18-A: "And I say unto thee, That thou art **Peter** *(Greek "petros," a small stone), and upon this* **rock** *(Greek "petra"),* **I will build my church.**"

(**Rock:** Greek 'petra," a great or large stone, that is referring back to Peter's answer to Jesus in verse 16 where Peter says, "Thou art the Christ the Son of the living God.")

As Pastor Don Farmer of West Virginia said,

"You can't build a church upon a small stone (Peter, Greek "petros" = a small stone), it must be upon a Large Rock as "petra," or Christ (Greek, "petra" = a great rock.

Bedrock" of Christianity

The "Bedrock" of Christianity is, **"CHRIST IS THE SON OF GOD,"** God incarnate in flesh.

Grossly Mistaken Identification

As an adjunct (a secondary thing added to another but not essential to it) to validate their religion, our Roman Catholic friends mistakenly believe that Peter is that rock on which the church was built. However, **all** true believers are referred to as lively (living) stones built up a spiritual house.

> *I Peter 2:5:* **Ye** (all believers) *also, as **lively** (living) **stones**, are built up a spiritual house, an holy priesthood, to offer up spiritual sacrifices, acceptable to God by Jesus Christ.*

Singular and Plurals in the King James Bible

NOTE: Ye: In the King James Bible, pronouns beginning with a "**y**" [**ye; you; your; yours; yourselves**] always refer to more than one person and is plural. Pronouns beginning with a "**t**" [**thou; thee; thy; thine; thyself**] always refer to only one person. **"You"** which can be singular or plural in modern English, is also in the King James Bible about 2,000 times.

Although believers are referred to as living stones, **Jesus Christ is the Great Rock** of our salvation.

Scriptures Declare Christ to be The Rock of Salvation

Peter knew that the church was **not** built upon himself:

> *I Peter 2:4: To whom coming (Jesus), as unto **a Living Stone**, disallowed indeed of men, but chosen of God, and precious.*

> *I Peter 2:6: Wherefore also it is contained in the Scripture, Behold, I lay in Sion **a Chief Corner Stone**, elect, precious: and he that believeth on him shall not be confounded.*

> *I Peter 2:7: Unto you therefore which believe he is precious: but unto them which be disobedient, The **Stone**, which the builders disallowed, the same is made **the Head of the corner**.*

> *I Peter 2:8: And **a Stone of stumbling**, and **a Rock of offence**, even to them, which stumble at the word, being disobedient: whereunto also they were appointed.*

Paul knew that the chief foundation was Jesus Christ:

*I Corinthians 3:11: For **other foundation** can no man lay than that is laid, which is Jesus Christ.*

*I Corinthians 10:4: And did all drink the same spiritual drink: for they drank of that **spiritual Rock** that followed them: and **that Rock was Christ**.*

*Ephesians 2:20: And are <u>built upon the foundation of the apostles and prophets</u>, **Jesus Christ himself being the chief Corner Stone.***

Matthew, Mark, and Luke knew that Jesus was the Stone:

*"The **Stone** which the builders rejected" - Matthew 21:42; Mark 12:10; Luke 20:17.*

The Old Testament writers referred to Messiah as The Rock and The Stone:

David prophesied:

*Psalms 18:31: For who is God save the LORD? or who is **a Rock** save our God?*

*Psalms 118:22: **The Stone** which the builders refused is become **the head Stone** of the corner.*

See also Psalms 18:2, 31, 46; 27:5; 28:1; 31:2, 3; 40:2; 42:9; 61:2, 6, 7; 71:3; 78:16, 20, 35; 81:16; 89:26; 92:15; 94:22; 95:1.

Isaiah refers to Messiah Jesus as a tried precious Corner Stone in Zion:

*Isaiah 28:16: Therefore thus saith the Lord GOD, Behold, I lay in Zion for a foundation a **Stone, a tried Stone, a precious Corner Stone, a sure foundation**; he that believeth shall not make haste.*

Moses knew that God was the Rock:

Deuteronomy 32:4: **He is the Rock**, *his work is perfect: for all his ways are judgment: a God of truth and without iniquity, just and right is he. (Of course, Jesus is God - I Timothy 3:16.)*

See also Deuteronomy 32:4, 15, 18, 30, 31.

Daniel prophesied of that "Great Stone" which was not cut out by hands:

Daniel 2:34 - that a **Stone** was cut out without hands

Daniel 2:35 - the **Stone** that smote the image became

Daniel 2:45 - the **Stone** was cut out of the mountain

Samuel referred to God as the Rock of Israel and salvation:

2 Samuel 22:47: "**...**the God of the **Rock** of my salvation."

2 Samuel 23:3: "**...**said, the **Rock** of Israel spake to me."

Jesus is the crowning achievement (**capstone**) of all prophecy (2 Peter 1:19; Philippians 2:9-11; Luke 24:13-27).

To many religionists, the "traditions of men" are equal to or more important than the Scriptures (Matthew. 15:3, 6; Mark 7:3; 7:8, 9; Colossians 2:8.)

Christ as the Rock to Other Entities

◆ Christ, as the Rock <u>to the Church,</u> was the foundation and **chief corner Stone -** (Ephesians 2:20).

◆ Christ, <u>to the unbelieving Jews,</u> was a **stumbling Stone -** (Romans 9:32, 33; I Corinthians 1:23)

◆ .Christ, <u>to Israel,</u> was the **Headstone** of the corner (Zechariah 4:7).

◆ Christ, <u>to the Gentiles,</u> was the **smiting Stone** cut out without hands - (Daniel 2:34).

◆ Christ, <u>to unbelievers,</u> is the **crushing Stone** of judgment - (Matthew 21:44).

◆ Christ, <u>to all who will drink,</u> was the **smitten Stone** that the Spirit of life may flow from Him (Exodus 17:6; John 4:13-14; 7:37-39; I Corinthians 10:4).

Paul said that James, Cephas (Peter), and John appeared to be pillars of the Early Church:

*Galatians 2:9: And when James, Cephas, and John, who seemed to be **pillars**, perceived the grace that was given unto me, they gave to me and Barnabas the right hands of fellowship; that we should go unto the heathen* (Gentiles), *and they unto the circumcision* (Jews).

Though Peter appeared to be a leader (spokesman) of the group, he was no greater pillar of the Church than was James (pastor of the Church at Jerusalem), John (beloved writer of five NT books), and Paul who wrote 13-14 NT books. It appears to this writer that **if** the Church were to be founded upon one spiritual man (as RC claims), it should be one that walked according to the truth of the Gospel. Only two verses after the above verse naming James, Peter, and John as seeming pillars of the Church, Paul (who wrote about half of the New Testament) rebuked Peter to the face because he was to be blamed (Galatians 2:11). The church was NOT founded upon a man. Even Paul's companion, Barnabas, was also carried away with their dissimulation (hypocrisy; deception; false appearance) - Galatians 2:13.

The Church's One Foundation

The "Church" cannot be built solely upon any ordinary sinful man; it is built upon "ONE," The God-man, the Lord Jesus Christ. The "household" of God is built upon the apostles (plural) and prophets (plural), **Jesus Christ himself being the chief corner stone.**

> *Ephesians 2:19-20: Now therefore <u>ye</u> (Gentiles; see verse 11) are no more strangers and foreigners, but fellow-citizens with the saints, and of the household of God; And are **built upon the foundation of the apostles and prophets**, **Jesus Christ himself being the chief corner stone**.*

The foundation of the apostles and prophets is in reference to the divine inspiration of the Scriptures...**THE WORD OF GOD**.

The foundation of the church is so plainly stated that even a child (Matthew 19:14), and a fool (Isaiah 35:8) know that Christ is the Rock of salvation.

That Rock was Christ (I Corinthians 10:4).

Israel Called the Church in the New Testament

The Greek word "ekklesia" (ek-klay-see'-ah) meaning "assembly" is used to refer to both Israel in the wilderness as well as to the New Testament Church in the world.

> *Acts 7:38: This is he* (Moses), *that was in the* **church** (Greek "ekklesia" = English "assembly") *in the wilderness with the angel which spake to him in the mount Sina, and with our fathers: who received the lively oracles to give unto us.*

Assembly: A called out people as was Israel of the OT. The NT Church in this dispensation of grace (age; economy; administration) is God's assembly of called out people that is comprised of both Jew and Gentile in the world but **called apart** from the world. These elect members are predestined to be conformed to the image of Christ - (Romans 8:29).

Observe that though God knew His believing children before the foundation of the world, they were not and are not predestined to salvation (or forced to be saved). They that do repent and believe the Gospel of Jesus Christ are predestined to be conformed to the image of

Christ. The elect children spoken of, whether of Israel or the NT Church, are already saved children of God, not unsaved candidates for salvation.

Probably the future church is referred to by Jesus in Matthew 18:17 as it had not yet been established. Both entities, Israel and the Church, are called apart upon to be a separate or "called out" assembly from the world.

How is the Church Distinguished from Israel?

The NT Church of the Gospel Age (Dispensation of Grace) could be likened as the Kingdom of Christ in mystery form (Matthew 13:11, 24, 31, 33, 44, 45, 47). God's Spirit indwells believers continually. Old Testament believers were indwelt of the Holy Spirit piece-meal and for a time only. Christ fulfilled the Law for believers and we are no longer under Mosaic Law (Romans 3:21, 28; 6:14, 15; Galatians 2:16, 21). Now in the dispensation of grace, "...For even Christ our Passover is sacrificed for us" - I Corinthians 5:7. Of course, our Lord Jesus fulfilled all the types and demands of the Law.

OT Israel was under the ceremonial Law of Moses. Unlike the New Testament Church, Israel was required to obey certain ceremonial laws requiring sacrificial offerings of an innocent animal's blood upon an altar and to observe set feasts (Leviticus 23), new moons, and other observances.

The Church Age is different from the Dispensation of OT Law

The Church Age is different from the Dispensation of OT Law and also the future **literal Kingdom of Christ** of which Jesus rules *outwardly* on the throne of David in Jerusalem. Jesus literally indwells and rules believers *inwardly* in the Dispensation of Grace.

Various Titles Applied to the New Testament Church Age

- The Dispensation of the Gospel (I Corinthians 9:17)

- The Dispensation of the Grace of God (Ephesians 3:2)

- **The Kingdom of Heaven** in mystery form (Matthew 13)

- The Age of Grace (John 1:17; Romans 6:14)

- The Mystery which hath been hid from ages and from generations (Colossians 1:26; Ephesians 3:2-6) which had not been revealed in OT times.

- The Dispensation of the Holy Spirit

Seven "Kingdom of Heaven" parables are given by Jesus in Matthew chapter 13 which appear to illustrate spiritual conditions of the Church Age. Others believe that the Kingdom of Heaven parables are restricted to the Millennium. However, it is no secret that Israel is to be the chief nation during the Millennium and there will be little need for parables, types, and figures. In Matthew chapter 13, Israel appears to be a "treasure hid in a field" (Exodus 19:5; Psalms 135:4; Matthew 13:44) as she now appears during the times of the Gentiles, largely still dispersed ("hidden") among many nations of which the Gentiles are chief nations. Again, the nation of Israel will be the chief nation during the Millennium. In this present Dispensation of Grace, **The Pearl of Great Price** (Matthew 13:45-46) appears to be the Church and again, **the Treasure Hid in a Field** appears to be Israel.

After the Church Age and the following 7-year Tribulation Period, there will be a literal 1,000-Year Kingdom-Rule of Jesus Christ in Jerusalem on the Throne of David.

Various Titles Given to the Millennial Age

- The Golden Age

- The Millennium

- The Restored Garden of Eden

- The Kingdom Age

- The Perfect Age (Others, as the writer, believe the Perfect Age follows the Millennium and earth's baptism of fire, Perhaps "ideal age" fits better)

- The Sabbath Age (7th- thousand-year period since creation)

- The Stone Kingdom

- Messiah's Kingdom

- Jesus' Reign on Earth

- The Throne of David

The word "millennium' (meaning one-thousand) refers to a special "thousand-year period." The word millennium itself does not occur in Scripture but the basis for its use in Revelation chapter 20 is the Greek word "chilioi" (khil'- ee-oy), meaning one-thousand.

The Millennial Reign of Christ:

- Christ's universal reign of peace and righteousness (Daniel 2:44)

- Christ will reign and execute justice and judgment in all the earth (Jeremiah 23:5).

- The King will be none other than the true Son of David (Luke 1:32; Isaiah 9:7).

- The Lord of Hosts shall reign from Jerusalem and before His ancients gloriously (Isaiah 24:23; Micah 4:7).

- The Kingdom will be set up forcibly by Christ Himself (not through preaching or any work of social reformation devised by man (Matthew 24:30).

- All earthly kingdoms will have to give way to His rule (Revelation 11:15; Zechariah 14:9; Psalms 72:11).

◆ Christ's dominion will be from sea to sea (Psalms 72:8; Zechariah 9:10).

◆ The Great Tribulation will come to its close with all offenders being banished before the Millennium begins (Isaiah 13:9).

◆ At the end of the Great Tribulation and before the beginning of the Millennium, the wheat and the tares of the gospel age will be separated by the angels (Matthew 13:30, 41).

◆ At the end of the Great Tribulation and before the beginning of the Millennium, the nations of earth will be thoroughly sifted (Joel 3:2, 12).

◆ Israel, after purification (Ezekiel 20:33-38; Amos 9:9-10), will be centered in Palestine (Ezekiel 20:40-44; 36:24; Amos 9:14, 15).

◆ Jerusalem will become the capital of the earth and the pride of all nations (Isaiah 60:14; 62:7; 65:18; Psalms 48:2; Jeremiah 31:23; Zechariah 8:3).

◆ The Lord will be in the midst of Jerusalem (Ezekiel 48:35; Joel 3:17, 21; Zephaniah 3:15-17; Zechariah 2:10).

◆ People of all nations will make pilgrimages to the world's capital for religious refreshment (Isaiah 2:1-3; Jeremiah 3:17; Micah 4:2; Zechariah 8:20-22; 14:16-19).

◆ During the Millennium, there will be no more heathen nations (Psalms 47:5-9).

◆ During the Millennium, justice will prevail and there are no oppressors (Psalms 72:1-8); all satanic opposition will be banished (Revelation 20:2.

◆ The Millennium will be a great age for the spread of God's truth (Psalms 85:11-13).

◆ There will be great changes in the animal kingdom (Isaiah 11:1-9; 35:9; Ezekiel 34:25-28).

- The curse will be removed from all nature (Romans 8:19-23) and the whole earth will become a watered garden (Isaiah 35:1-7).

- All the nations and all the ends of he earth shall see His salvation (Isaiah 52:10; 65:17-19; Zechariah 2:10-13).

- Longevity of life will be restored to terrestrial, earthly man (Isaiah 65:20).

- All will live comfortably and will be able to live in peace (Isaiah 65:21-25).

- All the implements of war in the world will be converted into constructive implements of work (Micah 4:3).

- Righteousness shall go before the King of Kings and shall set all men on earth in the way of His steps (Psalms 85:13).

CHAPTER 6

GOD IS NOT FINISHED WITH ISRAEL

God is not yet finished with Israel and she has a glorious future! In the end times, there will be two re-gatherings of the Jews, first in unbelief (which occurred in May 1948) and later in faith and Messianic acceptance (Ezekiel 37; Isaiah 11:11-12; Zephaniah 3:19-20). Presently, we are living in the "times of the Gentiles" (Luke 21:14) and also in the "Dispensation of the grace of God" which is the Church Age (Ephesians 3:2-7). The times of the Gentiles began after the reign of Israel's last king. The Church Age will end before the beginning of Daniel's Seventh Week of Prophecy (Titus 2:13; Revelation 3:10; 4:1; Romans 5:9; I Thessalonians 5:9; I Corinthians 15:51-58; I Thessalonians 4:13-18). This period of Daniel's 70th Week of Prophecy is Jewish time again (Daniel 9:24-27). After the end of the Church Age and the First Resurrection (translation; rapture), the Jews will be deluded into accepting a covenant with the false messiah (Daniel 9:27A) and confirm a 7-year pact with the master con man (antichrist). In the middle of the seven-year pact, this satanic indwelt man will break the pact with Israel and the Jews will undergo a 3 ½- year period of intense persecution called the "Time of Jacob's (Israel's) Trouble" (Jeremiah 30:7). At the conclusion of the Great Tribulation, all the nations of the world unite against Israel in a satanically conceived attempt to annihilate them from off the face of the earth (Joel 3:2; Zechariah 12:3; 14:2). That is the present goal of militant Islam. However, just before Israel's looming extinction, the remnant Jewish population will repent and accept Christ as Messiah (Zechariah 12:10) and all Israel will be saved. Christ will then set up His Millennial (1,000-year) Kingdom with Jerusalem as the capitol city (Zechariah 14:16) and the regathered remnant of believing Jews as the ruling nation (Isaiah 2:2-4; Jeremiah 31).

God has a special love for the Jews and they have always been "the apple of his eye" (Zechariah 2:8).

The Church

A basic but limited outline of the Church Age is also given in the 2nd and 3rd chapters of the book of Revelation. The writer believes that the Seven Churches *may* represent, broadly, seven overlapping periods of Church history. Undoubtedly, all of the conditions described for each of the Seven Churches are prevalent in many Churches during the entire Church Age and probably representative of all of today's churches. The writer believes that there is a correlation between Revelation chapters two and three and the seven Kingdom of Heaven parables of Matthew chapter 13 (the writer's opinion). Of course, Paul, Peter, and Jude tell us about the **last days** also, as well as the Master Prophet, Jesus

(**NOTE**: Although the "last days" apply to Jewish time, the Last Days can be applied to the end of the church age which ends right before the beginning of the Tribulation Period and can also refer to the last days of the times of the Gentile nations during The Tribulation Period which is called Daniel's 70th Week of Prophecy. Perhaps it can be better expressed by saying that we are in "the last days of the last days.")

Does the New Testament Church Replace Israel?

The false dogma of the Church replacing Israel is commonly labeled as "Replacement Theology." Although the NT Church includes Jews as well as Gentile believers, it is not a continuation or extension of *National Israel*. Actually, the Jews were the first members of the NT Church. Both the Church and Israel are "ekklesias" (assemblies; called-out entities; separate from the world). Israel and the NT Church are two separate entities. Again, Israel was under Mosaic Law and the NT Church is under the dispensation of **grace** (Ephesians 3:3; John 1:17; Romans 6:14). The civil and ceremonial laws, new moons, and dietary laws which were given to Israel under Mosaic Law are not binding to the Church. However, the moral laws have never been abrogated and are binding in every age and especially in the New Testament Church Age. Nine of the ten **OT Commandments** are repeated in the New Testament (Colossians 2:14, 16; Matthew 19:18-19; Romans 13:9; Galatians 5:19; Ephesians 4:25, 28; Ephesians 5:3; Revelation 21:8). Obedience to the **Sabbath Day Commandment** is not repeated or taught in the New Testament. The Mosaic Law observances (civil; ceremonial; new moons; Sabbaths; set feasts) are all fulfilled and abolished in Christ.

> *Colossians 2:14-17: Blotting out the handwriting of ordinances that was against us, which was contrary to us, and took it out of the way, nailing it to his cross; And having spoiled principalities and powers, he made a shew of them openly, triumphing over them in it. Let no man therefore judge you in meat, or in drink or in respect of an **holyday**, or of the **new moon**, or of the **sabbath days**: Which are a shadow of things to come; but the body is of Christ.*

The early church body was made up primarily of Jews; the latter church body is made up primarily of Gentiles.

One writer has said, "Believing saints in this church dispensation are in the middle of a Jewish Sandwich!"

In Romans chapter 9, <u>in the past</u>, the **Jews** rejected the Gospel. In Romans chapter 10, <u>in the present age</u>, repentant **Gentiles** respond affirmatively to the gospel and become part of God's family of saints. In Romans chapter 11, <u>in the future</u>, the **Jews** will receive the gospel

(**NOTE**: One of the best explanation addressing the Sabbath Day subject that this writer has come across is the excellent booklet, "Sunday or Sabbath" written by John R. Rice. The booklet is published by the *Sword of the Lord Publishers*, P.O. Box 1099, Murfreesboro, TN 37133. The writer has a file copy on his PC.)

CHAPTER 7

SIGNS OF THE TIMES

Many 'Signs of the Times' Prophetically Indicate the Last Days. Observe the Following Trends and Warnings:

- ➢ A reverse reformation is occurring in Protestant churches. Many Protestant leaders are aligning with The National Council of Churches and The World Council of Churches, which are apostate religious organizations. The One-World Church has already come into being. It was introduced in June 1997 as the United Religions Organization (URO). The church's charter was to have seen signed in June 2000, and by June 2005, the church hopes to be fully operational. The supporters say, "peace will be impossible without the **taming of fundamentalism** through a United Religion that professes faithfulness only 'to the **global spirituality** and to the health of this planet" (Emphasis added). Though it talks of peace, the URO has one basic agenda. It is to unite all people under one religion so that they will accept The New World Order, a One-World Government. A peace without God is a false peace - (Excerpts from, *The Sword of the Lord*, December 8, 2000, "Noteworthy News Notes," pp. 2, 10).

- ➢ Pastors (clothed as sheep, but actually goats) and *so-called* theologians are denying the resurrection and the deity of Christ.

- ➢ A few years ago, a *professor* (not possessor) of Furman University (then, a Baptist school) in Greenville, SC converted to Roman Catholicism. A few years earlier, during a public county school board meeting (the writer being present), the same professor zealously defended the acceptance of graphic pornographic literature for the curriculum of the local high schools. Dr. Smith appeared delighted in likening those of us who opposed the pornographic material as "Hitler and the Nazi regime censoring public books." When invited to openly read the *innocent trash* in the presence of a large gathering and with live television coverage, the religious Pharisee (wolf in sheep's clothing) declined.

Matthew 12:33 - The tree is known by his fruit

John 7:24 - Judge righteous judgment

Another one of the porno defenders was a school board member and a deacon in a church in the southwest area of Greenville. Apparently, he remained in good standing with his pastor and fellow church members. The writer would have refused to remain a member of a church that tolerated that deacon.

In several Protestant denominations (United Methodist; Presbyterian USA; Episcopal; Anglican; Lutheran; etc.), the proposal to endorse practicing sodomite (homosexual) ministers has been approved; however, the United Methodist has not yet officially endorsed practicing sodomite ministers, though they do allow them to minister in their churches. Some of these groups believe it is okay as long as the Sodomite preacher remains celibate (does not practice his sexual perversion). How ludicrous and absurd! For a professing Christian denomination to even consider the possibility of a Sodomite preacher is insane and unbelievable. Why would any blood-washed, born again Christians even consider it? Prostitutes and drunkards wallowing in their vomit know better.

(UPDATE: As of this date of November, 2011, The Presbyterian Church [PC/USA] has officially legalized sodomite [homosexual] ministers; so has the Anglican/Episcopal and the United Church of Christ [not The Church of Christ].

The writer anticipates that it will not be too long before the United Methodist Church does the same. As of June, 2019, the United Methodist Church, by a slim margin, rejected the endorsement of endorsing homosexual ministers)

Matthew 21:31: "...Verily I say unto you, That the publicans and the harlots go into the kingdom of God before you."

Is it not strange (not really) that "so-called" holy men of God possess the spiritual equivalence of demonic voodoo worshippers and the moral standards of barnyard farm animals?

Sodomy has found fertile soil in Christian America (so-called). The perverted life-style is called...gay rights (euphemism for sad rights); alternate life-style (perverted sexual behavior); domestic partners (queers); significant other (too shameful to name). These euphemisms that are used to soften the face of sins, are so incredulous that they are laughable, even to morons. What was the prevalent and prominent sin before the destruction of Sodom and Gomorrah and the World Flood? See Romans 1:23-27; Jude 7-8.

Sodomite priests and preachers are boldly coming out in the open (as NAMBLA or **N**orth **A**merican **M**an **B**oy **L**ove **A**ssociation)

It is not uncommon to see large groups of sodomite protesters in public demonstrations.

The Presbyterian Church office in Washington wants their members to push for state and federal laws to change in favor of "same gender unions" (*The Voice in the Wilderness*, Asheville, NC, October 2005)

The Presbyterian Church (USA) chose as one of their top officers a female pastor who believes in ordaining homosexuals and appointing them as church officers (The "Rev." Susan R. Andrews of Bethesda, Maryland (*The Biblical Evangelist*, July-August, 2003, page 14)

The Episcopal Church approved the consecration of an openly gay bishop on 8-5-03 at the church's national meeting in Minneapolis; the vote was 62 to 43. The Rev. Gene Robinson (bishop of the Diocese of New Hampshire, a 56 divorced father of two, had been living with his male partner for 13 years (*The Greenville News* of SC, August 6, 2003, p.1-a)

Recently, **Furman University** of Greenville, SC with a 175-year old Baptist tradition, voted to offer health insurance benefits to domestic partners and unions among people of the same sex (sodomites) and unmarried couples (adulterers shacking up). History professor, Lloyd Benson said, "In terms of the faculty, I don't think this is a very significant shift." For President David Shi said, the benefits issue "is not one of theology but one of equity for all Furman employees." (*The Greenville News*, pp. 1A, 3A, June 19, 2001).

The Dallas–based **Southern Methodist University** (SMU) - which is affiliated with the United Methodist Church (UMC)...announced...that the college will offer medical benefits and reduced tuition to the same-sex partners of employees starting next year, *The Dallas Morning News* reported. Morgan Olsen, an SMU administrator, said the benefits plan was "a good business decision that would allow SMU to remain competitive for top teaching talent" – *(THE SWORD OF THE LORD*, June 22, 2001, p. 10, *Noteworthy News Notes)*.

So much for contemporary heathen religion veiled in the garb of orthodox Christianity!

Large Companies are Now Jumping on the Bandwagon

Many large companies are now jumping on the bandwagon and awarding domestic partner insurance coverage for both straight (heterosexual) and sodomite (homosexual; sad; gay) partners.

Here are some other of America's companies who score "perfect" (100 %) with Sodomites:

-Adobe Systems	-American Airlines
-Aetna	-Anheuser-Busch
-American Express	-Apple Computer

-AT & T

-Bank of America

-Bell South

-Best Buy

-Boeing

-BP America

-Bristol-Myers Squibb

-Capital One

-Charles Schwab

-Chevron

-CIGNA

-Citigroup

-Clorox

-Coca-Cola

-Coors Brewing

-Corning

-Daimler-Chrysler

-Dell

-Dow Chemical

-DuPont

-Eastman Kodak

-Eli Lilly

-Ernst & Young

-Estee Lauder

-Fannie Mae

-Ford Motors

-General Mills

-General Motors

-Glaxo-Smith

-Google

-Hewlett-Packard

-Intel

-Honeywell International

-North America Insurance

-IBM

-Intuit

-Kraft Foods

-Lehman Brothers

-J. P. Morgan Chase & Co.

-Levi Strauss

-MetLife

-Johnson & Johnson

-Merrill Lynch

-Microsoft

-Motorola

-Nationwide

-NCRF Corp

-New York Times

-Nike

-Northrop Grumman

-Pepsico

-Pfizer

-Viacom

-Prudential Financial

-US Airways

-Visa International

-Volkswagen Of America

-Sun Microsystems

-Wachovia

-Walgreens

-Wells Fargo

-Whirlpool

-Xerox

-Walmart & Sam's

-McDonalds

-PriceWaterhouseCoopers

-Pillsbury Winthrop Shaw Pittman

-Home Depot

Since this list was compiled, many others have joined with the sodomite agenda.

A later un-validated report of March 2008 says that Ford Motor Co. has ceased to support gay (sad) rights. However, there are other reports that say Ford continues to support gay rights but on a lesser scale. Ditto for McDonalds.

(The following articles copied from *The Voice in the Wilderness*, January/February 2007, p. 13)

The United Church of Christ has recently accepted the **Cathedral of Hope** in Dallas, TX, to their denomination. The Cathedral of Hope is known as "the world's largest homosexual church." Senior pastor Jo Hudson (a female) has been a minister with the UCC since 1997. Since the 1970's, the UCC has been allowing homosexuals to be pastors and 2005 "officially endorsed same-sex marriage" - *World* 11/25/06.

Isn't this the same religion that Obama has joined?

➤ A new child's book about two penguins, "And Tango Makes Three," is based on two male penguins who adopted and raise a chick as their own in the Central Park Zoo in New York City. The zookeeper said the two penguins must be in love. School **Superintendent Filyaw** (of a concerned parent's child) considers the book, written for 4-8-year-old's, "adorable." The book has also created controversy in Savannah, Mo. - *The Washington Times* 11/27/06.

In Canada - A so-called "human-rights commission" in Canada recently ruled that an advertisement **quoting the Holy Bible was "hate speech" because it offended radical "gay" activists.** The Employment Non-Discrimination Act (ENDA) currently in the Senate could grant them that kind of power in the United States, too. – Beverly LaHaye (per her letter received and dated March 2007).

More American Down-Falls

Islamic Countries and Good Old USA (*The Perilous Times*, March/April, 2007, p. 6)

The following are the actual voting records of Arab and Islamic States as recorded in the U.S. State Dept. and at the United Nations, **Voting Against the U.S.:**

-Kuwait 67 % of the time	-Sudan 75 %
-Qatar 67 %	**-Pakistan 75 %**
-Morocco 70 %	-Libya 76 %
-Yemen 74 %	**-Egypt** 79 %
-United Arab Emirates 71 %	-Lebanon 80 %
-Jordan 73 %	**-India 81 %**
-Saudi Arabia 74 %	-Syria 84 %
-Oman 74 %	-Mauritania 87 %
-Algeria 74 %	

More Signs of the Times!

Here are examples of U.S. Foreign Aid to those who hate us (and Israel):

-Egypt receives $2,000,000,000 (two billion) per year

-Jordan receives $192,814,000 million annually

-Pakistan receives $6,721,000 million annually

-India receives $143,699,000 million annually

ARE WE CRAZY!?

God said to Jehoshaphat, "Shouldest thou help the ungodly?" Has there **ever** been a country as ours that treats its enemies so well? Did the reader observe the dominant religions of these countries? Is the reader aware of the religion of most terrorists? Islam is one of the bloodiest if not the bloodiest religion that has ever existed (see the writer's booklet, *ISLAM.*)

IRAQUI CASUALITIES VERSUS ILLEGAL ALIENS *(Perilous Times,* March/April, 2007)

According to Rep. Steve King ***of Iowa,***

-12 Americans are murdered every day by illegal aliens (That's 4,380 per year!). That's more than 21,000 murders by illegal aliens since September 11, 2001.

-13 people per day are killed by illegal alien drunk drivers (That's an additional 4,745 premature deaths per year). And liberals try to tell you that Iraq is a "quagmire."

-8 American children are molested by illegal aliens every day (That's 2,920 innocent children annually whose lives are ruined – by scum who wouldn't be prowling for American kids if the federal government enforced our immigration laws. (From Center for Individual Freedom)

Romans 13:12: ***The night is far spent, the day is at hand****: let us therefore cast off the works of darkness, and let us put on the armour of light.*

Considering that the book of Romans was written over 1,900 years ago, how much closer is the day at hand?

One major religious organization (RC) has many Sodomite priests as well as a large percentage of drunkards (euphemism = alcoholics). If the reader is unaware of these things, he is not well informed.

The NEA (National Education Association) is now promoting the homosexual life-style. It already approves of slaughtering unborn babies.

> ➤ A "cashless society" is imminently approaching us. We are inundated with plastic credit cards, bank debit cards, telephone **cards**, pre-paid purchasing cards (Viz., vending machines; gas pumps; groceries; et al) and electronic banking. In the future, it will be mandatory for social security retirees to "direct deposit" their retirement checks. It's just a matter of time until there will be introduced an "International Currency Unit" (ICU) or Amero currency, similar to Europe's Euro ECU currency.

The writer even imagines that there will be a future tri-lateral pact of North America composed of USA, Canada, and Mexico. Probably this will ultimately evolve into a western conglomeration including Central America and South America in order to compete with Europe's Euro, the ECU (European Currency Unit) economy. Eventually, most of these nations will be led by antichrist himself. Again, some have postulated that the American dollar will die and be replaced with a new currency called the "Amero."

In time, an international currency will be introduced to the world, called the **ICU** (International Currency Unit). The wealthy international bankers, liberal leaders, and spineless politicians with global mentalities are yielding to an antichrist spirit (I John 4:3, 6; 2 John 7, 9; Jude 4). They are working together behind the scenes to include America in the "International Community of Nations." This ungodly melding of America with nations of false gods will only serve to plunge America into a deeper morass of sin and idolatry than ever before. Again, the political leaders of the world have a "globalist" mind-set. They believe that mankind's basic problems can be resolved by bringing all nations together into a world community (ala Hillary's, "It takes a village"), thus removing obstacles and differences that beset the world. The world is rapidly becoming a "Global Community." (Out of curiosity, the writer randomly examined ten items at Walmart and found that all were stamped, "Made in China.") But the main problem does not lie within these differences of societies and cultures; consequently, a consolidation of world governments does not get to the core problem which is **sin**. The forming of an international government to solve the world problems is like applying a band-aid to cancer.

Denominations have Removed the "Blood' from the Song Books

➢ Some religious denominations have removed the "blood' from the song books and many removed the blood from the pulpit a long time ago. Even cult religions are being accepted as Christian among some "so-called" Christian denominations. **-The Evangelical Lutheran Church of America** [ELCA] and the **Lutheran Church Missouri Synod [LCMS]** have both eliminated the great evangelistic hymn "There is a Fountain Filled with Blood" from their new "Service" and "Worship" hymnals.

➢ By a vote of 173-22, "Clergy and lay members of the Episcopal diocese of San Joaquin voted to sever relationships with the **Episcopal Church in the USA**. The separation came over "disagreement about the role of gays and lesbians" in the Episcopal Church.

➢ Many Protestants, like their Catholic counterparts, have begun to teach that the Church ordinances (Communion and Baptism) are sacraments that merit or confirm salvation (actually, some Protestant denominations as well as some non-Protestant religions have always taught "sacramental salvation").

➢ At this writing, one writer said that Southern Baptists (not a Protestant denomination) now have 1,225 ordained women bishops and deacons. *The Baptist Bible Trumpet (*June 2002) of Laurens, SC, also lists 4,743 for UMC (Methodist); 2,419 for PCA (Presbyterian); 1,358 for Evangelical Lutheran; 1,803 for United Church of Christ. Of course, a pastor or bishop is to be male only. There are two places that men are to have the authority, the church and the home. The ordination of women into this office is contradicted by the Scriptures - (I Timothy 2:12-14; I Timothy 3:1-12; Titus 1:5; I Peter 3:1; I Corinthians 14:34-35; I Corinthians 11:2, 3; Matthew 13:33; Revelation 2:20)

➢ **Luis Palau's** recent Buenos Aires, Argentina "Celebration Festival" featured "hip-hop," "tango" and "hard rock" music for young people. As with all Palau "festivals" [His newly coined word to replace "evangelistic crusades"], the "celebration" was ecumenically sponsored.

➢ There are many modern English **per**-versions of the Bible. One version, the **New International Version (NIV)** either disclaims or deletes 17 entire verses in the New Testament. The deceptive translations and interpretations of these New Age Bible Versions are leading toward a global or international Bible to accommodate all religions and offend none.

➢ Since most of the world leaders have a "One-World Mentality," the word "Global" appears to be the most prominent international word in religion, as well as in politics and economics. Several religions have suggested a consolidation with Rome and the pope as their head. This may occur in the "not too distant" future. We know that in the New World Order, state and religion will merge under the iron hand of the antichrist and the false prophet of Revelation.

➢ Annually, many thousands (1.2-1.4 million) of **unborn children are legally slaughtered in abortion mills** or abortion shops (not abortion clinics; clinics are for healing and saving lives, not butchering and murdering). The latest count of documented abortions (2006) is at 48 million or the equivalent number of people in NC, SC, GA, FL, MS, and Alabama. Apparently, the Hippocratic Oath has little or no meaning to many modern-day medical doctors.

Hippocratic Oath: Code of Medical Ethics, "I will not give to a woman an instrument to produce abortion" – (*World Book Ency.*, Vol. 9, p. 227, Copyright 1980, U. S. A.)

The fact that any government would put a stamp of approval upon the slaughter of babies (*first, second, third trimester, partial birth, or post birth abortion*) advertises its spiritual barometer and boldly asserts the wickedness of the murderers. Abortion is a horrible and hideous sin before a righteous and holy God. The abortionists have a great price to pay for their abominable sin. The writer is sure that primary-grade children have more spiritual discernment than many of our elected political officials (and non-elected judges) concerning the **heathen butchery of the innocent unborn children**.

A person can get into deep trouble with the government for destroying an eagle's egg (unborn eaglet) but is licensed by our "paganized" government to murder unborn babies in abortion mills.

> **(Eagle's egg:** A 1972 law passed by Congress says that messing with an eagle's embryo can get you a year in jail and a fine of $5,000.)

There is more regard for the American "symbol" (unborn eagle) than for the unborn American baby. Infanticide (The slaughter of babies) is done under the guise of calling the unborn baby *a non-person* or *an impersonal blob of flesh.* The baby-butchers seek to sanitize the murder of the innocent babes of God's creation as simply "a woman's choice" or as others say, "pro-choice." Even the euphemism, "a woman's choice," is pure hype because the baby-butchers never argue in defense of the choice of life or adoption for the innocent baby but only for the right to abort (abort: euphemism for murder or kill). America is guilty of INFANTICIDE. Those who oppose the butchery of innocent babes in the womb and yet remain silent to the horrendous murders will also suffer in this world when the judgment of God comes.

In the past, a mother's womb was the safest place for a baby, but now it is the most dangerous place for a baby. A sad thing is that we have multitudes of people sitting on church pews (and preachers alike) who do not utter a single peep in protest of the **infanticide** of millions of innocent babies. Many primitive heathen have better morals than "so-called" Christian church members and preachers. Great numbers of professing Christians vote for politicians that are pro-murder advocates of the innocent unborn. Actually, the Democratic Party of America officially endorses "the right to choose" (Meaning the right to murder). Again, abortionists never argue in favor of the "right to life." The Democratic-Socialist Party also supports special homosexual rights. To be fair, the Republican Party is not far behind because it is laced with left-wing liberals (RINOs) also. Though there are pockets of Christianity in America, our nation is no longer Christian; it is become a heathen nation.

Isaiah 5:20: Woe unto them that call evil good, and good evil.

To those who might not understand this verse, it means that a curse is pronounced upon those who would pervert truth.

NOTE ON ABORTION: As previously stated, America slaughters about 1.2-1.4 million babies annually by calling it a "woman's choice." These are not "abortion clinics," they are "slaughter houses." Again, clinics are for healing, not murder.

Abortionists have murdered more Americans than all of those killed in America's wars.

US War Deaths vs. US Abortions:

Revolutionary War------4,435 deaths

War of 1812-------------2,260 deaths

Mexican War-----------13,283 deaths

Civil War--------------498,332 deaths

Spanish War------------2,446 deaths

World War I----------116,516 deaths

World War II----------405,399 deaths

Korean War------------36,913 deaths

Vietnam----------------58,177 deaths

Grenada----------------------19 deaths

Panama----------------------23 deaths

Persian Gulf---------------383 deaths

Somalia----------------------43 deaths

Haiti--------------------------4 deaths

Iraq----------------------3,000 (+)

TOTAL----------------1,138,233 deaths (**about number of annual abortions**)

But total abortions (36 years since Roe vs. Wade of 1973) is about **48 million** to date at this writing (update: over 60 million as of 2018).

If you vote for a pro-abortion candidate, you are part and parcel to the murder.

Congress funds **Planned Parenthood**. Of Planned Parenthood's total revenue of $810 million, $265 million came from taxpayers in the form of government grants and contracts.

In 2004 and 2005, **Planned Parenthood** received $551 million in governmental funding (our tax dollars).

In 2005, **Planned Parenthood** performed almost 250,000 abortions (steadily increasing since 1997).

Planned Parenthood has reportedly spent over $110 million of taxpayer money bringing lawsuit, challenging legislation and promoting their agenda. **Planned Parenthood** is the chief promoter of abortion in America. Planned Parenthood is the number one abortionist mill in America.

A person can get into deep trouble with the government for destroying an "eagle's egg" (unborn eaglet) but is licensed by government (paganized leadership) to murder unborn babies in abortion mills. Don't harm the whale, upset the butterfly nest, disturb the habitat of a monkey (your uncle, not mine), or be negligent about feeding the dog, but its OK to kill the innocent babe of the womb (in "so-called" Christian America).

MORE SIGNS OF THE TIMES!

It is no longer perilous times for the adult world but also for the unborn child. Most preachers are too spineless to speak out against pagan abortions. Some may preach against sin (generically) but many are afraid to put a specific name or label to it.

CHAPTER 8

FULFILLED PROPHECIES AND MATHEMATICAL PROBABILITIES

They Prove the Deity of Jesus Christ

Dave Hunt says, "The Old Testament contains more than 300 prophetic references to the coming Messiah that were fulfilled in the life, death, and the resurrection of Jesus. Sixty of these are considered to be major prophecies. If we eliminate 12 of these as within the power of Jesus and for His disciples to deliberately fulfill, that leaves 48. Professor Peter Stoner calculated the odds to be 10 to the 157th power that 48 such prophecies could be fulfilled by chance in Jesus Christ. In probability theory, it is generally agreed that any odds smaller than 10 to the fiftieth power are the same as zero. Since 10 to the 157th power is 10 to the 107th power (that's a 1 with 107 zeros after it) smaller than 10 to the 50th power, we can safely say that the fulfillment by Jesus of these 48 specific prophecies proved conclusively that He is the Messiah" *--(Peace, Prosperity, & The Coming Holocaust, p. 100)*. As one writer stated "an incomprehensible mathematical monstrosity."

Clarence Larkin says on page 6 of his book, *Dispensational Truth*, "If I were to predict an earthquake in Philadelphia next year the chance would be 1 in 2 that it would occur. If I should add another prediction, that it would be on the Fourth of July, the chance is decreased to 1 in 4. And if I add another detail, that it will be in the daytime, the chance then becomes 1 in 8. And if I should add a fourth detail the chance would be 1 in 32. And if the details were 10 in number, the chance would be 1 in 1024. Now there were 25 specific predictions made by the OT Prophets bearing on the betrayal, trial, death and burial of Jesus. These were uttered by different prophets during the period from B.C. 1000 to B.C. 500, yet they were all literally fulfilled in 24 hours in one person. According to the Law of "Compound Probabilities," there is one chance in 33,554,432 that these 25 predictions could be fulfilled as prophesied. If one prophet should make several predictions as to some one event, he might by collusion with others bring it to pass, but when a number of prophets, distributed over several centuries, give detailed and specific predictions as to some event, the charge of collusion cannot be sustained. It is a fact that there were 109 predictions literally fulfilled at Christ's First Advent in the flesh. Apply the Law of "Compound Probabilities" to this number, and the chance was only one in BILLIONS that they would be fulfilled in one person."

By using Larkin's method of calculating probabilities (doubling the probability for every prediction added), we obtain quite a large number. For the fulfilling the 109 predictions, the probability is, <u>one in </u>30 nonillion, 449 octillion, 666 septillion, 536 sextillion, 148 quintillion, 552 quadrillion, 852 trillion, 470 billion, 824 million, 435 thousand, 712 hundred.

This number is greater than 30 followed by 30 zeros.

William W. Orr said in his booklet, *Can we Be Sure Jesus Christ Is God*, "If you were to measure the chance that over 300 differing prophecies would happen to converge on one man, the law of probability would demand a sum calling for more zeros that there are letters in all the words of an unabridged dictionary!"

Consider the probabilities of these astronomical numbers:

➤ The probability that one man could fulfill **one** prophecy in 300 is *"one in 300."*

➤ The probability that one man could fulfill **two** prophecies in 300 is *"one in 90,000."*

➤ The probability that one man could fulfill **three** prophecies in 300 is *"one in 27 million"* ("one in 27,000,000").

> ➢ The probability that one man could fulfill **four** prophecies in 300 is *"one in 8 billion/100 million"* ("one in 8,100,000,000").

> ➢ The probability that one man could fulfill **five** prophecies in 300 is *"one in 2 trillion and 430 billion"* ("one in 2,430,000,000,000").

> ➢ The probability that one man could fulfill **six** prophecies in 300 is *"one in 729 trillion"* ("one in 729,000,000,000,000").

> ➢ The probability that one man could fulfill **seven** prophecies in 300 is *"one in 218 quadrillion and 700 trillion"* ("one in 218,700,000,000,000,000").

> ➢ The probability that one man could fulfill **eight** prophecies in 300 is *"one in 65 quintillion and 610 quadrillion"* ("one in 65,610,000,000,000,000,000").

> ➢ The probability that one man could fulfill **nine** prophecies in 300 is *"one in 19 sextillion and 683 quintillion"* ("one in 19,683,000,000,000,000,000,000").

> ➢ The probability that one man could fulfill **ten** prophecies in 300 is *"one in 5 septillion, 904 sextillion, and 900 quintillion"* ("one in 5,904,900,000,000,000,000,000,000").

Fulfilled Prophecies of Christ:

- His birth - Genesis 3:15; Daniel 9:26; Luke 2:11-20

- Place of His birth (Bethlehem) - Micah 5:2; Matthew 2:6; John 7:42

- Born of a virgin - Isaiah 7:14; Jeremiah 31:22; Matthew 1:23

- Be born the seed of Abraham - Genesis 22:18; Matthew 1:1-16

- Born of the lineage of the tribe of Judah (Juda or Judas) - Genesis 49:8; Matthew 1:3, 16; Luke 3:23, 33; Revelation 5:5

- Be called out of Egypt - Hosea 11:1; Matthew 2:15

- Heir to the throne of David - Isaiah 9:6, 7; Matthew 1:1

- Time of His first coming - Daniel 9:25; Galatians 4:4

- Praised by little children - Psalms 8:2; Matthew 21:4, 5

- Innocent children slaughtered because of a vile, jealous king - Jeremiah 31:15; Matthew 2:17

- Proclaim a jubilee to the world - Isaiah 58:6; 61:1; Luke 4:18, 19

- Dwell in Nazareth - Isaiah 11:1; Matthew 2:23

- Would be a prophet like Moses - Deuteronomy 18:15; Matthew 17:3; Luke 16:29, 31; 24:27, 44; John 1:17; 3:14; 5:46, 47

- Be a priest after the order of Melchizedek - Psalms 110:4; Hebrews 5:6; 6:20; 7:21

- Ministry in Galilee - Isaiah 9:2; Matthew 4:15

- His ministry one of healing - Isaiah 53:4; Matthew 8:17

- Declared to be the Son of God - Psalms 2:7; Matthew 4:6; 8:29; 14:33; 16:16; 27:43

- His ministry would be characterized by miracles - Isaiah 61:1; Luke 4:18, 19

- His miracles would not be believed - Isaiah 53:1; John 12:37, 38

- He would be zealous for His Father - Psalms 69:9; 119; 139; John 6:37-40

- Heralded by John the Baptist - Isaiah 40:3; Malachi 3:1; Matthew 11:10; Mark 1:2; Luke 7:27

- Anointed with the Spirit and to preach - Isaiah 61:1; Luke 4:16-21

- Filled with God's Spirit - Psalms 45:7; Isaiah 11:2; 61:1, 2; Luke 4:18, 19

- Adored by great men - Psalms 72:10; Matthew 2:1-11; 27:57, 58; John 3:1, 2

- Rides into Jerusalem upon a colt the foal of an ass - Isaiah 62:11; Psalms 118:26; Zechariah 9:9; Matthew 21:1-11

- He would heal many - Isaiah 53:4; Matthew 8:16, 17

- He would speak in parables - Isaiah 6:9, 10; Psalms 78:2; Matthew 13:10-15

- Rejected by His brethren - Psalms 69:8: John 7:3-5

- That He would be the rejected cornerstone - Isaiah 53:1; John 12:37, 38

- Rejected by the rulers - Isaiah 6:10; 29:13; 53:1; Psalms 69:4; Matthew 15:8, 9; 21:42; Luke 20:17

- Hated without a cause - Psalms 35:19; John 15:25

- Accused by false witnesses - Zechariah 13:7; Acts 1:9

- Betrayed by a friend - Psalms 41:9; John 13:18, 19

- Rejected - Isaiah 53:3; Matthew 27:22, 23, 25; Luke 23:18, 23

- Be sold for 30 pieces of silver - Zechariah 11:12; Matthew 26:15; 27:9, 10

- Betrayal price used to buy a Potter's Field - Zechariah 11:13; Matthew 27:7

- Forsaken by His disciples - Zechariah 13:7; Matthew 26:31, 56

- He would be a man of sorrows - Isaiah 53:3; Matthew 26:37, 38

- Be dumb before His accusers - Isaiah 53:7; Matthew 26:62; Mark 15:3-5; Luke 23:9; John 19:9; Acts 8:32, 33

- Be scourged, His face spit on, His hair plucked, His cheeks smitten - Isaiah 50:6; Matthew 26:67; 27:30; Mark 14:65; 15:19

- His garments parted and lots cast - Psalms 22:18; Matthew 27:35; Luke 23:34

- Surrounded and mocked by His enemies - Psalms 22:7, 8; Matthew 27:39-44; Mark 15:29-32

- People sit and stare - Psalms 22:17; Matthew 27:36

- Crucified between two thieves - Isaiah 53:12; Matthew 27:38; Mark 15:27

- They shoot out the lip, they shake the head - Psalms 22:7; 109:25; Matthew 27:39

- Hands and feet pierced - Psalms 22:16; Zechariah 12:10; 13:6; John 19:34; 20:25-27

- Agonize with thirst - Psalms 22:15; 69:3, 21; Matthew 27:34, 48; John 19:28

- Be given gall and vinegar to drink - Psalms 69:21; Matthew 27:34; John 19:29

- Not a bone of His body broken - Psalms 34:20; Exodus 12:46; Numbers 9:12; John 19:36

- Made intercession for murderers - Isaiah 53:12; Luke 23:32

- Dying Words foretold - Psalms 22:1; 31:5; Matthew 27:46; Mark 15:34; Luke

  23:46

- Willingly gave up His life – Psalms 50:6; 53:12; Daniel 9:26; Matthew 20:28; John 10:11, 18; Galatians 2:20; I

Corinthians 15:3; Hebrews 1:3; I Peter 2:24; Revelation 1:5

♦ Forsaken by God - Psalms 22:1; Matthew 27:46

♦ Cut off - Daniel 9:26; I Corinthians 15:3, 4; I Timothy 3:16

♦ Crucified Christ hidden by darkness - Amos 8:9; Psalms 22:2; Matthew 27:45

♦ Buried in a rich man's tomb – Isaiah 53:9; Matthew 27:57-60

♦ His body would not disintegrate - Psalms 16:10; Acts 2:27

♦ His resurrection foretold - Isaiah 26:19; Psalms 16:10, 11; Luke 24:17

♦ His ascension foretold - Psalms 68:18; 110:1; Mark 16:9, 14-19

♦ He would become a greater high priest than Aaron - Psalms 110:4; Hebrews 5:4-6, 10; 7:11-28

♦ He would be seated at God's right hand - Psalms 110:1; Matthew 22:44; Hebrews 10:12, 13

♦ Conversion of Gentiles unto Him - Isaiah 11:10; Romans 15:12

♦ His rejection would be followed by the destruction of Jerusalem and great tribulation - Daniel 9:27; 11:31; 12:1, 11; Matthew 24:15; Mark 13:14; Luke 21:20

The writer has not attempted to locate all 333 prophecies relating to the First Advent of Christ (Viz., birth; life; death; resurrection; et al), but he is aware of about 100 of them. Even if there were only 100 prophecies fulfilled, the chances that only 10 out of the 100 being fulfilled would be *"one in 100 quintillion,"* (one in 100,000,000,000,000,000,000").

Only the God-Man, the Lord Jesus Christ, could accomplish this.

The prophecy of **Psalms 22:16** says, *"They pierced My hands and My feet."* This is a prophecy of Christ's crucifixion which was written about 1,000 years before His crucifixion. Crucifixion was unknown then and was not invented until hundreds of years later. Crucifixion came into its earliest use with the Phoenicians, Greeks, Carthaginians, and Romans. Emperor Constantine, the first official pope (pontifex maximus), did away with it.

Prophecy of the suffering Savior is also found in **Isaiah 53:7; Daniel 9:28.**

The "Tree" (or, "Cross") of Christ's Crucifixion is Prophesied in OT Typology

Exodus 15:25: And he (Moses) *cried unto the LORD; and the LORD shewed him **a tree**, which when he had cast into the waters, <u>the waters were made sweet</u>: there he made for them a statue and ordinance, and there he proved them.*

The fulfillment (antitype) of the OT **tree** (type) is referred to several times in the New Testament (of course, the cross is synonymous with tree). The literal fulfillment is recorded in the four Gospels.

*Acts 5:30-31: The God of our fathers raised up Jesus, whom ye slew and hanged on **a tree**. Him hath God exalted with his right hand to be a Prince and a Saviour, for to give repentance to Israel, and forgiveness of sins.*

*I Peter 2:24: Who His own self bare our sins in His own body on **the tree**, that we, being dead to sins, should live unto righteousness by whose stripes ye were healed.*

*Acts 13:29-30: And when they had fulfilled all that was written of Him, they took him down from **the*** *tree, and laid Him in a sepulcher. But God raised Him from the dead.*

*Galatians 3:13: Christ hath redeemed us from the curse of the law, being made a curse for us: for it is written, Cursed is every one that hangeth on **a tree**.*

The bitter sufferings of Christ upon the **tree** (the wooden cross) is God's offering for our sins (John 3:16; 2 Peter 3:9) and sweetens the sorrows of our lives.

QUESTION:

Is there any human being of Jewish ancestry (Genesis 12:1-3; 28:10-15) of the tribe of Judah (Genesis 49:10) and of the family of David (2 Samuel 7:16; Jeremiah 23:56), born in Bethlehem (Micah 5:2; Matthew 2:16) to a Jewish virgin (Isaiah 7:14; Matthew 1:23) and who was despised and rejected by his own brethren (Isaiah 52:13-14; 53:1-9) and died being innocent (Luke 23:41; 2 Corinthians 5:21) and all of this before the destruction of the Second Jewish Temple (John 2:19-20)?

Prophecy foretold the TIME of Christ's of birth as well as the PLACE of His birth.

The PLACE of Christ's birth

The PLACE of Christ's birth was expressly stated to be in Bethlehem: See Micah 5:2; John 7:42; Luke 2:4. Bethlehem was also known as Ephrath (Genesis 35:19; 48:7); Beth-lehem-judah (I Samuel 17:12); Beth-lehem Ephratah (Micah 5:2); Bethlehem of Judea (Matthew 2:1); the city of David (Luke 2:4; John 7:42). See also Ruth 1:2; 4:11; Psalms 132:6.

Micah 5:2: But thou, Bethlehem Ephratah, though thou be little among the thousands of Judah, yet out of thee shall He come forth unto me that is to be ruler in Israel; whose goings forth have been from of old, from everlasting.

Jesus' birthplace is called Bethlehem "of Judea" to distinguish it from another city of the same name in the land of Zebulun (Joshua 19:15).

Bethlehem signifies "the house of bread," the fittest place for the true manna to be born, who is the Bread that came down from Heaven.

The TIME of Christ's First Coming

The TIME of Christ's First Coming would require a person to be a student of Scriptures. An outline of Jewish history that announced the First Coming of the Jewish Messiah is given in the Old Testament book of Daniel:

> *Daniel 9:24-27:* **Seventy weeks (490 years; seventy sevens = 490 years)** *are determined upon thy people (Jews) and upon thy holy city (Jerusalem), to finish the transgression, and to make an end of sins, and to make reconciliation for iniquity, and to bring in everlasting righteousness, and to seal up the vision and prophecy, and to anoint the most Holy. Know therefore and understand, that from the going forth of the commandment to restore and to build Jerusalem unto the* **Messiah the Prince** *shall be* **seven weeks (49 years), and threescore and two weeks (434 years):** *the street shall be built again, and the wall, even in troublous times. And after* **threescore and two weeks** *shall* **Messiah be cut off**, *but not for Himself: and the people of the prince (man of sin, the son of perdition) that shall come shall destroy the city and the sanctuary; and the end thereof shall be with a flood, and unto the end of the war desolations are determined. And he (antichrist) shall confirm the covenant with many (Jew and Gentile) for* **one week (7 years):** *and in the* **midst of the week (3 ½ years)** *he shall cause the sacrifice and the oblation to cease, and for the overspreading of abominations he shall make it desolate, even until*

the consummation, and that determined shall be poured upon the desolate.

To understand the length of Daniel's seventy weeks (or one week), we must understand Jewish prophetic time. We can determine this from comparing various Scriptures.

- In **Genesis 29:27**, Rachel's week is "seven other years."

- In **Numbers 14:34**, one day equals one year.

- In **Ezekiel 4:3-6**, we have a day for each year.

Daniel, who outlined Jewish history (Daniel 9:24-27), also used the time-year formula of a time being equal to one-year (Daniel 12:7). Adding 49 years + 62 years + 1 year = 490 years, which is equal to Daniel's seventy weeks of prophecy. Consequently, **the Jewish prophetic week equals seven years** (or one day equals one year). Also refer to Revelation 11:2 (42 months); Revelation 12:6 (1,260 days); Revelation 13:5 (42 months).

The Bible says that One Day with the Lord is as a Thousand Years:

*2 Peter 3:8: But, beloved, be not ignorant of this one thing, that **one day is with the Lord as a thousand years**, and a thousand years as one day.*

God is not locked into time and He owns it all. This reference in 2 Peter is in context a reference to "The Comings of Christ," and not a specific formula for prophecy. The past, the present, and the future are all known to God and appear to Him in the present tense. By studying the entire chapter, it can easily be seen that this verse is in answer to scoffers and unbelievers who doubted God's Word and His comings. The unbelievers loved to ridicule the prophets of God concerning their prophecies of the Lord's coming. God will fulfill His promise of "coming" when it pleases Him to do so, not to satisfy the scoffers.

*2 Peter 3:3-4: Knowing this first, that there shall come in the last days **scoffers**, walking after their* *own lusts, And saying, **Where is the promise of His coming?** For since the fathers fell asleep, all things continue as they were from the beginning of the creation.*

Presently, we are in the times of the Gentiles (Luke 21:24)   The times of the Gentiles will coincide and end with the end of Daniel's 70th Week of Prophecy (Luke 21;20-28).

Jewish Bible prophecy is "One day for a Year or One week for 7 Years."

In Revelation 11:3, we have 1,260 days representing the Great Tribulation. The duration of the Great Tribulation is 3 ½ years, which is ½ of one week or ½ of seven years. The Great Tribulation Period is referred to in Daniel 12:7 -- "...it shall be for a time (one year), times (two years), and an half" (½ year), or 3½ years. The "times" formula of the Great Tribulation is further substantiated in Daniel 4:16, 23, 25, 32; 7:25; 12:7; Revelation 12:14.

(**NOTE**: The Jewish calendar was made up of 12 months of 30 days each. We presently observe time by the Gregorian calendar. "Thirty days hath September, April, June and November; all the rest have thirty-one, except February which has 28." Of course, every four years. February has a day added, hence, February 29, or "leap year.")

The last-half of Daniel's 70th Week (3 ½ years) is also referred to in the following references:

Revelation 11:2 (42 months); Revelation 12:6 (1,260 days); Revelation 13:5 (42 months).

Using the formula of "one week equals seven years," the length of the seventy weeks of Jewish prophecy, historically, is seventy sevens (70 X 7) or 490 years.

The Jews had disobeyed God's order to observe a "year of rest" unto the land every seventh year when they entered the promised land - (Leviticus 26:34-35). For disobeying and for their idolatrous sins, God decreed that Israel would go into captivity to the Babylonians for seventy years (Jeremiah 25:9). This "Seventy Years of Captivity" corresponded to the neglect of the seventy years of rest for the land and the seventy weeks of years determined by Daniel's prophecy (or 490 years of Jewish history). The 490 years of Jewish history divided by every 7th year of neglect equals seventy years of the Jews punishment in Babylonian captivity.

(**NOTE**: Interestingly, Jesus told Peter, a Jew, that the Law of Forgiveness for sin against a brother who would sin against him was seventy times seven or 490 times [Matthew 18:21-22]. Of course, this definite number is an expression of an indefinite number of times of forgiveness.)

The Jews of the Old Testament knew the month and day (Nisan 14) of the Passover Sacrifice. An observant Jew would easily recognize that the innocent, substitutionary animal sacrifice was a type of the future "once and no more" perfect sacrifice to be fulfilled in the person of the Jewish Messiah (Christ our Passover is sacrificed for us (I Corinthians 5:7). We know that Jesus fulfilled the typology of the Passover Lamb that pictured Himself as the Lamb of God that taketh away the sin of the world (John 1:29; Revelation 5:6). The Jews were to observe the Passover on Abib (Nisan) 14, at even (3:00-6:00 PM). So any student of Old Testament Scriptures (Daniel 9:25-26) could easily count from the "going forth" of the Persian decree of Nehemiah 21-8 (about 436-445 BC) to restore and build Jerusalem unto Messiah the Prince. We are told that it would be "Seven Weeks and Threescore and Two weeks," or 69 weeks that equaled 483 years. Again, the Jewish prophetical week equals seven years, or a year for each day.

Reviewing the Seventy Weeks Of Daniel's Prophecy in their chronological order, we have:

1.) At the end of the Seven Weeks of the Persian decree (7 X 7 = 49 years), Jerusalem is restored.

2) At the end of the Seven Weeks and the Sixty-Two Weeks (69 weeks plus 7 weeks of years = 483 years) of the Persian decree, Messiah comes and is cut off.

These two segments of time may have run concurrently, without a time gap.

3) After allowing for a long gap of time between the 7 Weeks plus the 62 Weeks (483 years), the final one-week (seven years) of Daniel's 70 weeks is the Tribulation Period of which the last one-half (3 ½ years) is The Great Tribulation.

The prophet Jeremiah calls the final week of Daniel's prophecy, "the time of Jacob's (Israel's) trouble" - (Jeremiah 30:7).

(**NOTE**: One Bible scholar said, "It appears that the beginnings of these three segments of time began on sabbatical cycles, not just a random time.")

The promised Jewish Messiah was to come and be cut off at the end of the first two periods of time of Daniel's 70 Weeks of Prophecy – (Daniel 9:24-27). This would have been 483 years from the "going forth" to fulfill Cyrus'/Artaxerxes' decree of 444-445 BC to rebuild and restore Jerusalem which action began about 436 BC. This time, properly accounted, brings us to the time AD 30-33 of Christ and His crucifixion. The sacrificial feast of the Passover clearly pointed to the 14th day of the first Jewish month of the Jewish Messiah's crucifixion.

Why did the Jews not know of the very season that Messiah was to come? The answer lies in the Jews rejection of the Word of the Lord (Isaiah 28:11-12; I Corinthians 14:21). In other words, they listened to the Talmud (writings of religious leaders, especially **Maimonides)** instead of the Hebrew Scriptures. The Jews substituted the Talmud and allowed traditions (Mark 7:13) to take the place and authority of the Holy Scriptures.

(**Maimonides**, [my MAHN ih deez], 1135-1204, was a Jewish philosopher. His principal philosophical work, *The Guide of the Perplexed*, completed in 1,190, was an attempt to harmonize Judaism with the teachings of Aristotle. It influenced theologians like Thomas Acquinas because of its use of Aristotle's doctrines. Maimonides was a rabbi. His full name was Moses ben Maimon. He wrote many works on law, logic, astronomy, and medicine - *World Book Ency.*, M volume 13, Copyright 1980.)

However, there was a small remnant that waited on and expected the Messiah's coming into the world. The Holy Ghost was upon Simeon and he waited for the consolation of Israel (Luke 2:25). God has always had a remnant of believers in every age and they are usually a very small minority.

> *Luke 2:26: And it was revealed unto him* (Simeon)
> *by the Holy Ghost, that he should not see death,*
> *before he had seen the Lord's Christ.*

Tradition says that Simeon was expert in the Scriptures and the first doctor of law to receive the title of *rabban* (rabbi; teacher). It also appears that Anna, *a prophetess*, had been expecting the Messiah (Luke 2:36-38). Jesus' coming was also known by Jesus' foster-father Joseph, His mother Mary, and Mary's cousin, Elisabeth, and her husband, Zacharias. John the Baptist also knew of Jesus' coming.

When observing international mind-sets of world leaders (politics; religion; economics) and the American government's attitude toward **fundamentalist** Bible-believers, the writer is inclined to believe that we are very close to the beginning of Daniel's 70th Week of Prophecy. This is very near to the First Resurrection (translation; rapture) of the Church that occurs right before the beginning of "The Time of Jacob's Trouble (Daniel's 70th Week of Prophecy; The 7-Year Tribulation Period). This Tribulation Period of the 7-Year Tribulation Period is, "...the coming of the great and dreadful day of the LORD" - Malachi 4:5.

(**Fundamentalist:** Fundamentalist Bible-believers are not remotely related to the versions of "fundamentalists" portrayed by mass news media and journalists. Through despite or ignorance [or both], the media has attempted to label genuine Bible believers as purveyors of terrorist acts such as those committed by cults, fanatical occults, radical Muslims, and lunatic kooks. False religion also perpetrated great slaughter in the name of Christianity [See Fox's Book of Martyrs; History of the Baptists, et al]. The carnal media does not know the difference between the genuine and the phony. Actually, born-again fundamentalist Christians are the most gentle, loyal, and patriotic citizens in America, in spite of public and governmental disdain for it.)

CHAPTER 9

THE LUMINARIES PROPHESY CHRIST AND HIS REDEMPTION

Job, which is probably the oldest book of the Bible, refers to the constellations of the solar zodiac:

Job 9:9: Which maketh Arcturus, Orion, and Pleiades, and their chambers of the south.

Even before the Holy Scriptures were given to man on earth, the heavens declared the glory of God (Psalms 19:1) in "star-pictures." Before Abraham's time, Job referred to the Mazzaroth, or Constellations of the Zodiac (Job 38:32).

(**NOTE**: Not only is the Book of Job probably the oldest Book in the world, but it is also considered the most scientific book of the Bible. However, there are those that believe that the book of Enoch to be the oldest book in the world though it is not accepted as inspired of God.)

The star-pictures of the Zodiac (in the beginning of creation) were prophecies in the heavens concerning Christ, His wounded heel (sufferings for our sin), conquest of Satan (wounding Satan's head), redemption for man (Calvary), and His eternal Kingdom.

Of course, the Constellations have been grossly misinterpreted and counterfeited by astrologers, corrupt religionists, humanists, and promoters of classic mythology. It is **not** hard to figure out the symbolism of "Leo the Lion" (Revelation 5:5), "Virgo the Virgin" (Isaiah 7:14; Matthew 1:23), and "Hydra the Serpent" (Genesis 3:1, 4; Revelation 12:3, 9; Revelation 20:2).

A **star** (or, "perhaps" an angel) heralded the birth of the King of the Jews to the Magi of the East (Matthew 2:1-2). God garnished the heavens with groups of stars that send the greatest message of all time (The Gospel of the Saviour of the world) to all men everywhere. Even a fool should be able to reason that the star-designs of heaven brilliantly and majestically declare the greatness and glory of God.

Remember too, a fool in Scriptures is not someone who is mentally deficient, but an unbeliever who is proud, spiritually blind, stubborn, and independent of God (sound like anyone you have known).

Latter-Day False Prophecies

Examples of False Prophecies: (Copied from *Message of the Christian Jew,* May-June 1998, pp. 1, 3, 8, 9, *Some Prophecies that Never Came True,* Dave Hunt.)

- **Pope Gregory XI's** papal bull of 1372 pronounced papal dominion over the entire Christian world, and in 1568, Pope Pius V swore that it was to remain an eternal law. In 1870, two months after the Vatican pronounced papal infallibility, Rome was liberated from papal dominion by Italy's army and Pope Pius IX took refuge in the Vatican.

- **Nostradamus** (Michel de Notredame) - 1503-1566) predicted that the world would end in 1886.

(Nostradamus was a French **astrologer** and physician. His prophecies were vague and open to many interpretations - *World Book Encyclopedia*, 1980, Vol. 14, page 428.)

The Bible condemns the works of **astrologers** (Isaiah 47:13; Daniel 1:20; 2:2, 27; 4:7; 5:7, 11, 15)

- **Sun Myung Moon** prophesied decades ago that he would take over the world.

- **Herbert W. Armstrong** predicted that his Worldwide Church of God would be raptured to the ancient city of Petra in 1972 and Christ would return in 1975.

- **Elijah Mohammed** prophesied to his Black Muslim followers in the 1970's that God's return to North America was imminent.

- **Joseph Smith** prophesied that the United States would suffer unparalleled multiple disasters (pestilence, hail, famine, and earthquake) which would sweep the wicked (non-Mormons) off the land, leaving Mormons safe in their Zion haven in Missouri. Instead, they fled to Utah.

- **Brigham Young** prophesied that the Civil War would not free the slaves.

- **Charles T. Russell** (JW) declared that the Second Coming had taken place invisibly in October 1874 and that in 1914 the faithful (the 144,000) would be translated to Heaven. He also said that Armageddon (which began in 1874) would culminate in 1914 and the end of the world.

- **Jehovah Witnesses**, in the early 1920's, zealously distributed on the streets and from door-to-door, a book entitled *"Millions Now Living Will Never Die."* It was prophesied, "The year 1925 is a date definitely and clearly marked in the Scriptures, even more clearly that that of 1914...we may confidently expect that 1925 will mark the return of Abraham, Isaac, Jacob, and the faithful prophets of old...to the condition of human perfection." The JW's even built a house in San Diego where the patriarchs were to live and tried to deed it to King David (The house was quietly sold in 1954). In 1966, the Watchtower Society published, *Life Everlasting In Freedom of the Sons of God.* On page 29, this book stated that 1975 would be the end of 6,000 years of mankind's existence on earth. From 1966 to 1974, the Watchtower consistently taught that "the end" was near. In the March 1968 edition of Our Kingdom Ministries the Watchtower Society stated that Armageddon would begin in 90 months. They quoted 'experts" who stated that the nations gathering nuclear stockpiles would be out of control by 1975 and civil unrest would be the order of the day. Thousands of Witnesses sold their homes and property, quit their jobs, quit school and even sold their businesses in preparation for "the end." But what was the Watchtower Society doing during in 1975? That same year they bought and began remodeling an expensive property in New York City. October came and went and nothing happened. Hundreds of thousands of disenchanted Witnesses left the Watchtower organization. Although the Watchtower taught that 1975 would be the end, they blamed their followers for the failed prophecy. The June 22, 1995 *Awake* magazine states: "The wrong conclusions were due to a fervent desire to realize the fulfillment of God's promises in their own time." What a clever spin! Only the very naïve would swallow this. In 1982, the Watchtower was still selling the 1975 Yearbook of Jehovah's Witnesses which taught that 1975 was the end. Finally, the Watchtower Society admitted in the March 22, 1993 *Awake* magazine that the writings in the Watchtower magazine were not "inspired and infallible and without mistakes." Imagine the financial ruin of those who sold their homes and property because of those uninspired prophecies. ...losing everything and then being blamed for the failed prophecy. (For documentation consult: *Our Kingdom Ministry*, March 1968 p.3; *Kingdom Ministry*, May 1974; *Kingdom Ministry*, June 1978 p. 1; *Awake!*, June 22, 1995 p. 9; *Kingdom Ministry*, p. 4; *Awake!* March 22, 1993.)

- **William Miller** (SDA) predicted that Christ would return in 1843 and then revised to October 22, 1844. Miller admitted his error.

- **Ellen G. White** (SDA) who had repeatedly endorsed Miller's prophecy, insisted that Christ had indeed come, but not to earth. Instead, He had entered the holy of holies in Heaven to make an atonement for all that are shown to be entitled to its benefits. Her "entitled" of course meant "salvation by works."

- **Kenneth Copeland** prophesied: "As you move into **the month of January (1976), you** shall see more of the outpouring of God's glory than...in the history of this world...limbs that have been amputated put back on by the power of God...instantly...bald men's hair grow to a full head of hair...eyeballs replaced where there were no eyeballs...God will cause your automobile...that gets 10 miles to the gallon to get 70 miles...the same old car!"

- **Benny Hinn** said on December 31, 1989, "The Lord also tells me...**about '94 or '95**, no later than that, God will destroy the homosexual community of America...by fire...Canada will be visited with a mighty revival that will start on the west coast of British Columbia...in the next three years."

- **Daniel Logan** known as, "the reluctant prophet," predicted that the Vietnam War would continue from 1965 to 1985 and the U.S. and Russia would become allies against China before 1980.

- **Astrologers** predicted the communist government in China would fall by 1970.

    (Astrology is a universal practice in pagan religions. It is as old as the Tower of Babel where the Chaldeans surveyed the stars for a sign (Genesis 11.)

- The <u>stargazers</u> predicted President Kennedy's reelection rather than his assassination.

- **Astrologers** assured England that she would **not** be involved in World War II.

    (Fifty-three percent of Americans believe in some form of astrology. Over two thousand newspapers carry a daily horoscope.)

- **Astrologers** predicted that California would slide into the sea in 1969.

    (The Bible warns that people will give heed to seducing spirits and doctrines of the Devil...as we await the Second Coming of Christ.)

- **Evangelist Harold Camping**, of the California based Christian Network Family (on the air since 1958), has three times falsely predicted the world would end. He claimed he knew a special numerical system based on the Bible which indicated the occurrence of certain great religious events including the Great Flood, the Crucifixion, and the Second Coming of Jesus Christ. Camping's false predictions include September 6, 1994; May 21, 2011; June 7 2013 (The Sword of the Lord, June 7, 2013, p. 19).

(The following excerpts concerning Benny Hinn are taken from, *The Bible For Today*, B.F.T. #2784, October-December 1997, *"Benny Hinn's Move Into Necromancy,"* by Richard Fisher with M. Kurt Goedelman)

- **Benny Hinn** has long been infatuated with the late faith healer, Kathryn Kuhlman. In his "Partner Conference" in Atlanta and to those viewing the June 11, 1997 installment of his daily "This is Your Day" program, he stated "The Lord showed me a vision...I saw myself walk into a room and there stood Kathryn Kuhlman...she said, 'Follow me'...And I followed her to a second room. In that second room stood the Lord...when I saw the Lord, Kathryn disappeared...And now the Lord looked at me and said, 'Follow me.' And I followed him to a third room. In the third room sat a gentleman...in this wheelchair...a big hole in his neck...A tube down his throat...tubes down his body. Totally crippled...paralyzed...And now as the man was healed, the Lord looked at me with piercing eyes and said, Do it!'...and the dream and the vision came to an end...It was Kathryn Kuhlman who took me, who introduced me to the Holy Spirit.

(The following is copied from *"Message of the Christian Jew,"* dated May-June 1998, *"Some Prophecies That Never Came True,"* by Dave Hunt, pp. 1, 3, 8, 9.)

Hinn said, "I got saved in Israel in 1968"... in "PTL Family Devotion." Hinn said, "It was in Canada that I was born again right after "68," ...in a 1983 St. Louis message. Hinn says he was converted in 1972, during his senior year in high school...in "Good Morning, Holy Spirit." <u>But</u> he dropped out before his senior year.

QUESTION: When was Hinn saved? Or how many times? (Note: Our *Arminian* brethren think that sinners can be saved, lost, and re-saved over and over again, thus crucifying the Lord anew. In his defense, perhaps Hinn is alluding to multiple salvations; however, God only gives *eternal* life "once.")

In Orlando on December 31, 1989, Hinn said, "**The mid '90s will see a new move of God to shake the world with the last great revival. Many will be raised from the dead**. Angels will come knocking at your door...An earthquake will hit the east coast of America and destroy much in the '90s. Not one place will be safe in America from earthquakes in the '90s."

<u>The following is taken from *The Voice in the Wilderness* monthly publication, pp. 4, 5, February 2002, P.O. Box 7037, Asheville, NC 28802</u>:

A man Hinn had "slain in the Spirit" fell on a prostrate elderly woman and broke her hip, resulting in her death.

At a South Africa crusade a man collapsed; Hinn said the Lord told him the man would be okay, but he died in the ambulance.

In 1993 in Basel, Switzerland, Hinn prophesied over a man with cancer that he had many years to live. He died two days later.

In Nairobi, Kenya early in May 2000, four patients released from a hospital to attend Hinn's "Miracle Crusade" died while waiting for prayer.

In a guttural voice, **Hinn arrogantly curses those who dare to question him**, curses their children and threaten that if he had a "Holy Ghost machine gun" he'd "mow down" critics.

95

According to the *The Voice in the Wilderness*, Benny **Hinn scorned doctrine as "sick stuff"** and said, "I don't discuss doctrine." Even TBN's **Paul Crouch** referred to sound doctrine as "doctrinal doodoo."

(**NOTE:** If you do not have doctrine [teaching; Bible truth], you do not have a foundation - Proverbs 4:2; Isaiah 28:9; 29:24; Matthew 7:28; Mark 1:22; 4:2; 12:38; Luke 4:32; John 7:17; Acts 2:42; 5:28; 13:12; Romans 6:17; I Corinthians 14:6; I Timothy 1:3, 10; 4:6, 13, 16; 5:17; 6:1, 3; 2 Timothy 3:16; 4:2, 3; Titus 1:9; 2:1, 7, 10; 2 John 9-10.)

In <u>Hinn's</u> Honolulu Crusade, he lured the audience with his revelations of not only Kuhlman but the Old Testament prophet Elijah. "I have not just seen angels, I've seen saints"...I've walked in the supernatural world...I've had individuals appear to me in my room. Not only angels...I was in prayer one day and a man appeared in front of me...And I spoke out and I said, 'Lord, who is this man I see?..I know you may---you may think I lost my mind, but the Lord said, 'Elijah the prophet'.

If we believe Hinn's words, it appears that he has had more visions than "John the Revelator."

<u>Ancient Israel had the same problems with false prophets and false visions even as we do today:</u>

*Ezekiel 13:3: Thus saith the Lord GOD; Woe unto the foolish prophets, that **follow their own spirit**, and **have seen nothing**!*

*Ezekiel 13:6-7: They have seen **vanity and lying divination**, saying, The LORD saith: and **the LORD hath not sent them**: and they have made others to hope that they would confirm the word. Have ye not <u>seen a vain vision</u>, and have ye not **spoken a lying divination**, whereas ye say, The LORD saith it; albeit **I have not spoken**?*

According to a Dallas-based organization known as *Trinity Foundation*, a watchdog group for televangelist, any time somebody on Hinn's Board of Directors disagrees with Hinn, he changes the board. Trinity Foundation has criticized Hinn for his lavish lifestyle, which includes a $10 million parsonage in California. "Can you imagine…spending $11,000 a night for a hotel room when you're on a side trip and charging it to the ministry?" Trinity Foundation president, Ole Anthony, asks. "Are thousands and thousands of dollars given to his wife and kids to go on shopping sprees? This isn't the way of God's people, " he contends. (*Agape Press*, Allie Martin, 7/8/2005, http://headllines.agapepress.org/archive/7/72005e.asp)

Once when a reporter was questioning Hinn about his expensive automobile, Hinn replied, "What, do you want me to drive a Volkswagen?"

(The followed copied from *The Voice in the Wilderness*, page 14, May 2005, www.thevoiceinthewilderness.org)

- **Kathryn Kuhlman** – In his book Healing: *A Doctor in Search of a Miracle*, **Dr. William Nolen** dedicates an entire chapter to his experiences investigating Kuhlman's healing crusades. Though sympathetic to Kuhlman as a person, Nolen was unable to document medically even one case of physical healing. At the time of his investigation, Dr. Nolen was chief of surgery at Meeker County Hospital in Litchfield, Minnesota. In his book *Occult ABC*, **Kurt Koch** described his own research into Kuhlman's healing ministry. He carefully followed up on a list of 28 cases of alleged healings in Minneapolis, Minnesota. "Ten had not been healed, seven had experienced an improvement in their condition, eleven had diseases in which the mind can play an important part. In the whole of this extensive report, there is not one clear case of healing from an organic disease" *fridaynews/wayoflife.org*
- */4/4/05*

- **One preacher** (initials E.V.) well known for his prophecy seminars, predicted a certain time of Christ's return in the 1980's (name withheld because of the lack of written documentation). The writer is not saying that this man was not saved, but he was carried away with his own fantasies.

- There are those who counted **Jeanne Dixon's prophecies** and concluded that she had a prediction accuracy percentage rate that was lower than most Wall Street stock brokers. <u>Jeanne luckily (or with the assistance of demons) and accurately predicted some major events:</u> - *Jeane Dixon: The Washington Prophetess*, <u>By Noel Smith:</u>

In 1966 she told a newspaper reporter that Jawaharial Nehru would be succeeded as Prime Minister of India within approximately seven years by a man whose name began with the letter "S." On May 27, 1964, the intellectual Nehru died, and he was succeeded by Lal Bahadur Shastri.

In 1952 Mrs. Dixon described the President who would be elected in 1960. The description fit John F. Kennedy, and perfectly. And she predicted that that President would die a violent death while in office. She predicted that President Kennedy would be shot while in office; and she vainly sought to persuade some of his friends to get him to cancel his trip to Texas.

In June 1953 she said that Chief Justice Fred M. Vinson would die within a few months. He died suddenly the following September.

On June 19, 1964, she saw another tragedy in the Kennedy family. She vainly tried to persuade friends of Senator Ted Kennedy to keep him out of airplanes. A plane in which he was a passenger crashed on that day, and we all know the tragic consequences to the Senator.

In December 1963, when the strutting Nikita Khrushchev was to all appearances the master of Soviet Russian and her slave states, and would continue to be the master as long as the scoundrel wished, Mrs. Dixon said that Khrushchev would "shortly" be disposed. He was disposed the following October, and he has remained disposed. Since that October we haven't heard so much as a squeak form him.

In the fall of 1944 Franklin D. Roosevelt asked Mrs. Dixon to come to the White House. He asked her how much time he had left to finish his work. She told him six months or less. He died at Warm Springs, Georgia, on April 12, 1945.

When Prime Minister Winston Churchill was in Washington on an official visit in 1945, Mrs. Dixon told him that if he called the election that he had decided to call, he would be turned out of office. But she also told him that after six years he would be back as Prime Minister. "England will never let me down," he replied in the gruff Churchillian manner. Churchill called the election. England turned him out and put Clem Attlee in. Six years later Churchill was again Prime Minister.

In 1962 Mrs. Dixon said that Churchill would die at the end of 1964. She missed it twenty-six days.

She told Vice President Harry Truman that he would become President "through an act of God."

Mrs. Dixon said that the "symbols" told her that Fidel Castro believed that President Kennedy and Khrushchev were planning to eliminate him and replace him with somebody more to the liking of the United States and the United Nations. Therefore Castro arranged the assassination and Oswald was his trigger-man. She said that others were involved in the plot. <u>She also missed quite a few. Mrs. Dixon admitted that her predictions are not always correct.</u>

<u>EXAMPLES:</u>

She predicted that World War III would begin in 1954.

Red China would be admitted to the United Nations in 1958, yet this did not occur until 1971.

The Vietnam War would end in 1966, yet it did not end until 1975.

She predicted that Union Leader, Walter Reuther, would run for President in 1964, which he did not do.

Jeane predicted that Castro would be overthrown from Cuba in 1970.

 Jeane predicted that Russia would be the first nation to put a man on the moon.

On October 19, 1968, she predicted Jacqueline Kennedy was not thinking of marriage and the next day Mrs. Kennedy married Aristotle Onassis. (McDowell & Stewart, *Handbook of Today's Religions*," pp. 183-184, Thomas Nelson Publishers, 1983.)

<u>Jeane Dixon speaks nothing about the Lord Jesus Christ, nor sin, salvation, and judgment.</u> Mrs. Dixon, a devout Roman Catholic, said that during her visions she is "so filled with the glory of God" that she wants to give everything to everyone (Jeane did not charge for her services). She believed that her powers were a gift from God and refers to Paul's words in First Corinthians 1.

Mrs. Dixon didn't begin her career as a prophetess on her knees before God, with the open Bible as her guide. She began it at the steps of the covered wagon of a gypsy fortune-teller, with a crystal ball as her guide.

Mrs. Dixon has nothing to say about Jesus Christ, The Son of God, the "image of the invisible God, the first born of every creature."

Mrs. Dixon has nothing to say about Christ's substitutionary death, nothing to say about the absolute necessity of that death, nothing to say about His resurrection, nothing to say about His ascension...Nothing at all about Jesus Christ. Jesus Christ is the central theme of the prophets of God. Jesus Christ is the central theme of both the Old and New

Testaments. And His substitutionary death for sinners is the center of the central theme.

It only takes one of Jeanne Dixon's visions to set off an alarm bell: It is in Washington shortly after a humid midnight on July 14, 1952. Mrs. Dixon is in bed, "drowsy but not asleep." She has a sheet across her body. Suddenly she feels a motion against the mattress "to the left of my head." She rolls onto the left side, facing the east. She sees the body, but neither the head or tail, of a snake. It is "no bigger around than a garden hose." She feels the "powerful little body: twisting down the side of her bed and raising the mattress at the foot. She seems "cloaked in a substance as soft as eiderdown." She feels the snake's head "nudging" beneath her ankles. Its body grows larger as it wraps itself around her legs and hips. The snake gradually entwines itself around her chest. She sees its head but not the eyes. The snake has become about as "big around as a man's arm." The snake slowly turns its eyes and gazes into Mrs. Dixon's. "In them was the all-knowing wisdom of the ages." The snake is "vividly colored in yellow and black," has great jowls like miniature pyramids." The snake turns its eyes toward the east, and then turns its eyes toward Mrs. Dixon..."I sensed that it was telling me that if my faith was great enough I could penetrate some of this divine wisdom. I knew that I had God's protection, for the steady gaze of the reptile was permeated with love, goodness, strength, and knowledge. A sense of 'peace on earth, good will toward men's coursed through my being.

The Bible tells us about another lady, **Eve**, deceived by the serpent in the Book of Genesis. God has not called angels, apostates, nor snakes to reveal prophecy to us. His Words are finalized in the Book of Revelation.

-See Hebrews 1:2; John 1:1-2, 14; Revelation 22:19.

(**NOTE:** Roman Catholicism's "Mary worship" was established by Cardinal Benedetto Odescalchi, the first pope with the name of Innocent XI, when he initiated THE WORSHIP OF THE IMAGE, placed on the altar in 1677, and wanted his heart to be buried here, and not in the main chapel. This is placed on a plaque in the Chapel of the Virgin of the Grace at Saints Vincent and Anastasius.)

CHPATER 10

WHAT OF THE CORRECT EXTRA-BIBLICAL PREDICTIONS?

A false prophet (or anyone) may accurately predict events but their predictions must be rejected unless they are meticulously **true to Scriptures**, giving all honor to Christ as Creator, Savior, and Lord. Besides this, the Scriptures indicate that the prophecies of God received by men directly (future forecasting) would be "done away."

> *I Corinthians 13:9-10: For we know **in part**, and we prophesy **in part**. But when that which is **perfect** is come (completed canon of Scriptures), then that which is **in part** (sign gifts) shall be **done away**.*

Prophecies remained **in part** (I Corinthians 13:10) until John concluded the book of Revelation. The Word of God contains all of the prophecy that God pleases to reveal to us. Many "self-serving" preachers seek spiritual recognition for themselves at the expense of making revealed Scriptures of less importance.

> *I Corinthians 13:8: Charity never faileth: **but whether there be prophecies, they shall fail**; whether there be tongues, they shall cease: whether there be knowledge, it shall vanish away.*

> *John 4:48: The said Jesus unto him, Except ye see signs and wonders, ye will not believe.*

God greatly honors His name (Psalms 111:9), but *He magnifies His Word* (the Scriptures) *above His own Name*

> *Psalms 138:2: I will worship toward thy holy temple, and praise thy name for thy lovingkindness and for thy truth: for **thou hast magnified thy word above all thy name**.*

Anyone may predict the outcome of certain events (especially when there are only two outcomes; there is an easy 50:50 chance) but that does not make him/her a prophet or prophetess.

An ingenious scam artist in a large northern city (NYC, the writer thinks) devised a clever fast "get rich" scheme. Using the huge city phone directory, the scam artist selected a large pool of names at random. He then sent one-half of the selected pool of names one of two opponent's name as a winner and the other one-half pool of names, the other opponent's name as the winner. Of course, the scammer only chose events that involved two opponents (Viz., boxing matches; political elections; sporting events; et al). In this way, he was always sure to have a 100% accuracy rate of half of the selected pool of names. The scammer would then continue the cycle of sending winner predictions to the 50 % that had chosen the correct winner. Of course, the scammer would request money from those winners who had received the correct predictions in order for them to receive more "correct" future predictions. Yes, he got caught.

Even a blind hog might root up an acorn every now and then.

Charismatic Leaders Muddy the Waters

- "Jesus was not God and never claimed to be." - (Charismatic--**PC**). Anyone making such a statement does not know God.

- "His physical death (shedding of blood) could not save you." - (Charismatic--**KH**) Apparently this charismatic is not very familiar with Scriptures (Hebrews 9:22).

- "He was not begotten until He was born again in hell." - (Charismatic - **KH**). Jesus did not need to be born again, He is God in flesh. Jesus was begotten in His resurrection from the dead (Psalms 2:7).

- "I could have done the same thing Jesus did if I had known the Word of God as He did." - (Charismatic--**KC**).

What a crazy statement! (Excerpts taken from *The End Times & Victorious Living* newspaper a ministry of the Paw Creek Church and Media Ministry of Charlotte, NC, dated May/June, 2001)

So much for foolish charismatic gibberish!

• Charismatic writers **Clinton and Sarah Utterback** publish a devotional guide entitled *Horizons Unlimited*. In their lead editorial of the March, April, May 2005 issue, they say, "The passages in this devotional are drawn from words the Lord has spoken to me in my daily fellowship with Him. I know they are divinely inspired because of what Jesus said in John 10:27: 'My sheep hear my voice, and I know them, and they follow me.' More than twenty years ago, I was prompted by this verse to begin to train myself to be able to distinguish the voice of the Lord from all other voices." - *(The Sword of The Lord,* May 6, 2005, p. 7)

• **Jack and Rexella Van Impe:** *(The Biblical Evangelist,* July-August 2005, p.10). On Jack's April 16, 2005 broadcast, Rexella started the program with the announcement that Pope John Paul was in Heaven (Of course, this is contrary to Roman doctrine, which teaches that all Catholics, since none is perfect, must go to Purgatory first – a doctrine that vilifies and insults the finished work of Christ). Jack was careful to say he had read over 500 sermons by John Paul and they were all inspiring and biblical...Roman Catholics uphold the dogma that **their church is the sole path** to spiritual salvation for all humanity (for which John Paul II explicitly approved). Jack really waxed eloquent about what a defender of "the Faith" John Paul was, emphasizing that he insisted grace, through faith in Christ, was the only way to Heaven. Is that true? Of course not! On his six trips to the United States, speaking to the faithful masses in Chicago, John Paul declared: "By the Sacrament of Baptism we have been truly incorporated into the crucified and glorified Christ." When John Paul was in Washington, D.C, he led the faithful in prayer, intoning, "Through the intercession of Our Lady of the Rosary, whose feast we celebrate today, may we come one day to the fullness of eternal life in Christ Jesus our Lord, Amen."

Since Van Impe believes in biblical creation, he might want to think through what John Paul II said about Catholicism and evolution being "compatible." As recently as 1996 he sent a formal statement to the Pontifical Academy of Sciences stating that, "fresh knowledge leads to recognition of the theory of evolution as more than just a hypothesis." In short, John Paul wasn't any better as a scientist than he was a theologian.

It appears that it is wrong for those "right-wing Fundamentalists," who lack love, to sneer at false teachers, false religions, and compromisers, but it is okay to sneer at those Fundamentalists (as Jack does).

Jack's father was saved out of Roman Catholicism and preached hard and heavy against that religion during his entire ministry.

The editor of The Biblical Evangelist, Robert Sumner (who has been a long-time friend of Jack), says that he would not be surprised if Jack converted to Roman Catholicism.

The writer believes that it is very confusing and harmful to new Christians and babes in Christ when well-known religious figures within Christendom endorse leaders of religious orders that are laced with false doctrines and pagan practices.

(**NOTE:** The writer harbors no ill feelings towards Jack Van Impe. As the manager of a Dry Cleaner during the late 1960's, this writer felt it a privilege to assist in doing some of Van Impe's dry cleaning [free of charge of course] during his two-week city-wide crusade meetings at the Memorial Auditorium in Greenville, SC. Jack Van Impe died in January or February of 2020)

How to Identify a False Prophet

Deuteronomy 18:20-22: But <u>the prophet, which shall presume to speak a word in my name</u>, which

*I have not commanded him to speak, or that shall speak in the name of other gods, even that prophet shall die. And if thou say in thine heart, How shall we know the word which the LORD hath not spoken? When a prophet speaketh in the name of the LORD**, if the thing follow not, nor come to pass**, that is the thing which the LORD hath not spoken, **but the prophet hath spoken it presumptuously**: thou shalt not be afraid of him.*

*Matthew 7:15-16: Beware of **false prophets**, which <u>come to you in sheep's clothing</u>, but inwardly they are ravening wolves. Ye shall know them <u>by their fruits</u>. Do men gather grapes of thorns or figs of thistles?*

Matthew 15:9: But in vain they do worship me, <u>teaching for doctrines the commandments of men</u>

*Matthew 24:24: For there shall arise false Christs, and **false prophets**, and shall shew great signs and wonders; insomuch that, if it were possible, they shall deceive the very elect.*

I Peter 2:1: But there were false prophets also among the people, even <u>as there shall be false teachers among you,</u> who privily (secretly) shall bring in damnable heresies, even denying the Lord that bought them, and bring upon themselves swift destruction.

*John 4:1: Beloved, believe not every spirit, but try the spirits whether they are of God: because **many false prophets** are gone out into the world.*

*John 7: Many **deceivers** are entered into the world, who confess not that Jesus Christ is come in the flesh. This is a deceiver and an antichrist.*

Jude 4: There are certain men crept in unawares, who were before of old ordained to this condemnation, ungodly men, turning the grace of our God into lasciviousness, and denying the only Lord God, and our Lord Jesus Christ.

There were warnings in the OT against false prophets turning people to other gods – Deuteronomy 13:1-5; 18:20-22).

There were those with familiar spirits that peeped and muttered (Isaiah 8:19).

> *Isaiah 8:20: To the law and to the testimony: if they speak not <u>according to this word</u>, it is because there is no light in them.*

For "True" Believers:

- ➤ There is **no priest but Christ;**

- ➤ **No sacrifice but Calvary;**

- ➤ **No confessional but the Throne of Grace;**

- ➤ **No authority but the Word of God.**

What of Contemporary Healing Zealots?

Even, the religious Pharisees had a great **zeal** for God, but not according to the true knowledge or of salvation.

> *Romans 10:2: For I bear them record that they (religious Israelites) have a **zeal** of God, but not according to knowledge.*

> *Matthew 7:22-23: Many will say unto me in that day, Lord, Lord, have we not prophesied in thy name? and in thy name have cast out devils? And in thy name done many wonderful works?*

> *Matthew 5:20: For I say unto you, That except your righteousness shall exceed the righteousness of the scribes and Pharisees, ye shall in no case enter into the kingdom of heaven.*

Many of the modern-day **prophecy-faith-healers** claim that a person must be saved and filled with the Spirit of God in order to be healed. This may be the case sometimes but it was not always true. The blind man that Jesus healed had not even experienced the salvation of God.

(**Prophecy-faith-healers:** The writer calls them "prophecy-faith-healers" simply because most of the "so-called" healers claim to prophesy new and divine revelations "directly" from God. God's divine and final revelations are given to us in His Word. Of course, this is not to say that the Holy Spirit cannot impress us in certain matters of God's divine will.)

Actually, the healed blind beggar did not know the true identity of Jesus:

> *John 9:25: He answered and said, Whether he (Jesus) be a sinner or no, I know not: one thing I know, that, whereas I was blind, now I see.*

Before and after he was healed, the blind man did not know that Jesus was the promised Messiah, the Son Of God:

> *John 9:35b, 36-37: And when he (Jesus) had found him (the blind man that he had healed), He said unto him, **Dost thou believe on the Son of God?** He answered and said, **Who is he, Lord, that I might believe on him?** And Jesus said unto him, Thou hast both seen Him, and it is He that talketh with thee.*

From the record, we see that the blind man was not a saved man seeking out Jesus to be healed. It appears that Jesus went to the blind beggar who did not even know that Jesus was God manifest in the flesh. To excuse their failures, many modern-day healers use the catch phrase, *"You have to have enough faith to be healed"*. Though the blind man had faith enough to obey Jesus' instruction to go and wash in the pool of Siloam and then come seeing, he definitely was not a saint of God, filled with the Spirit. The writer believes that the overwhelming majority of those who received healing by Jesus and the apostles were not even saved people at the time of their healing. Since the natural man (an unsaved person - I Corinthians 2:14) receives not the things of the Spirit of God, wherein did **faith** rest and upon whom?

However, a lack of faith on the part of **the healer** was the problem at times (Matthew 17:19, 20).

(**Faith:** Faith was definitely a prerequisite at certain times and for certain situations - Matthew 9:20; Romans 12:6.)

The truth of the razzle-dazzle promotions of TV healers is that they are religious charlatans aiming at the pocketbooks of unsuspecting pawns

> *Matthew 7:22-23: Many will say unto me in that day, Lord, Lord, have we not **prophesied in thy name**? and **in thy name have cast out devils**? and **in thy name done many wonderful works**? And then will I profess unto them, **I never knew you**, depart from me, ye that work iniquity.*

This is a shocking expose' of religious people claiming to perform miraculous works! God openly exposes these unsaved religious satanic workings. Jesus said, "I never knew you". Who are the unsaved religious leaders among God's people today that are claiming to cast out devils (exorcism) and claiming to perform many wonderful works? The reader has the spiritual freedom to decide if today's actions are of God or of a secular and satanic origin.

During the Tribulation Period, the world will be deluded by the miracles of the antichrist's number one henchman, the beast out of the earth (Revelation 13:13-15). This miracle working religious leader of the world is called the "false prophet" in Revelation 13:13-14; 16:13; 19:20; 20:10. Most, including Catholic scholars, consider the false prophet to be the final pope.

Sin Is Not Always the Cause of Physical Sickness:

> *John 9:3: Jesus answered, **Neither hath this man sinned, nor his parents**: but that the works of God should be made manifest in him.*

The healing ministry of the apostles was unique to the time. **This marvelous healing power was not given to believers of every age.** The apostles were endowed with healing power for the purpose of authenticating their work and confirming the Gospel message - (2 Corinthians 12:12; Mark 3:14-15; Acts 2:43; 4:33: 5:12, 15; 19:12). By these miracles, the apostles were identified as apostles of Christ. If anyone would seek healing, they should obey the instructions of James 5:14.

One Christian writer has said, "Once a building (the Church) has been established, the scaffolds (authenticating charismatic gifts and miracles) are no longer needed."

We have many today claiming that they are apostles of Jesus Christ. Now apostles were sometimes referred to as disciples, but disciples are not necessarily apostles in the same sense as the chosen 12 apostles.

<u>There were at least three qualifications to be an apostle:</u>

1.) An apostles had to be **directly chosen** by Christ Himself

2.) An apostles had the **gift of healing and casting out demons**

3.) An apostle was an **eye-witness of Jesus' resurrection**.

Some add that an apostle also had to be a Jewish male and that Luke was a Gentile; however Luke was not an apostle (the writer believes that Luke probably was a Jew).

CHAPTER 11

SIGNS AND WONDERS

The gift of speaking in tongues (*foreign languages previously unknown to the speaker*) was a *sign-gift* of God to His **unbelieving** national people, the **Jews** (I Corinthians 14:22) which was prophesied in the OT (I Corinthians 14:21). God did not intend for sign miracles (Viz., healings; tongues; miracles; knowledge; et al) to always continue. God expects us to walk by faith and to study, meditate, trust, and cling to the His Word. Generally, wicked people seek after signs. The just are saved "through faith," shall "live by faith," and "walk by" faith - (Ephesians 2:8; Romans 1:17; 14:23; 2 Corinthians 5:7; I Corinthians 13:13).

> *Matthew 12:38-39: Then certain of the scribes and of the Pharisees answered, saying, Master, we would see a sign form thee. But He answered and said unto them,* ***An evil and adulterous generation seeketh after a sign****; and there shall no sign be given to it, but the sign of the prophet Jonas.*

The writer does not limit the working of the miraculous power of God to any age in history. The writer believes that God is sovereign and may miraculously heal people today in answer to prayer. It is interesting to note that in 6,000 years of Bible history, miracles **in abundance** only occurred in three brief periods of time: 1) Moses and Joshua; 2.) Elijah and Elisha; 3) Christ and His apostles and disciples.

On two occasions, the writer pointed out to charismatic brethren that an "abundance" of miracles occurred only within certain periods of time. When the writer also asserted that God desired that we believers should live by faith and not sight, the charismatics became very upset. To give them the benefit of misunderstanding "living by faith," perhaps they mistakenly thought that the writer was limiting God's power to perform miracles and miraculously heal the sick. The writer admits that he would love to see a miracle of instant healing or an appearance of an angel but also acknowledges the Scriptural injunction that says that a "wicked generation" seeketh after a sign. This does not limit God in working a miracle whenever it pleases Him. We cannot put God in a framework of opionated parameters and say that He can or cannot do a miraculous work in a certain dispensation or age. But by listening to some of today's professing healers, you would think that copious miracles of instantaneous physical healings were flowing from their their healing lines.

Isn't it strange (not really) that these healing miracles are absent in Shriner's Hospital, Nursing Homes, and the Hospital ER Rooms on Saturday nights where they are so greatly needed? God does not expect us to thrive upon miracles, but He does expect us to live by faith (Habakkuk 2:4; Romans 1:17; 5:1-2).

Even during the time of Jesus upon earth, John the Baptist did no miracle (John 10:41). Jesus said that among them that are born of women there hath not risen a greater than John the Baptist (Matthew 11:11). This is a rebuke to phony healers of today.

Again, "The just shall live by faith"

(Romans 1:17) A wicked and adulterous generation seeketh after a sign (Matthew 16:4).

The great apostle Paul besought the Lord thrice to be healed of a thorn in the flesh but God would not heal him. The Lord answered that His grace was sufficient for Paul.

Although Paul had raised Eutychus from the dead (Acts 20:9-11), he did not or could not heal Timothy's stomach. Paul instructed Timothy to use a little wine (unfermented grape juice) for the stomach's sake. The great apostle to the NT (Paul) also left Trophimus at Miletum sick (2 Timothy 4:20).

(Note: As modern medical doctors know, the acidic nature of grape juice aids digestion; whereas fermented "alcoholic" wine irritates the stomach lining as well as killing brain cells.)

Many of today's healers boldly advertise their specialty night for miracles and healings. The writer believes in "Show and Tell" or "Put Up or Shut Up." Consequently, over the years, the writer has invited self-acclaimed healers to Greenville, SC to heal children at Shriner's Hospital as well as older folk in nursing homes. In the early invitations, a chaplain of Shriner's Hospital gave the writer permission to invite healers to enter the hospital and heal the crippled. No one would respond to the invitation. WHY???

Raising the Dead

From Genesis to Revelation, we are told of only ten individual people who were raised from the dead.

In the Old Testament:

- Elijah raised the son of the widow of Zarephath (I Kings 17:22)

- Elisha raised the son of the Shunamite woman (2 Kings 4:32-36)

- The man cast into the sepulchre of Elisha (2 Kings 13:21)

In the New Testament:

- Peter raised Tabitha/Dorcas (Acts 9:40-41)

- Paul raised Eutychus (Acts 20:9-12)

Of course, these all were raised by the power of God, not by mere men.

Christ raised three (3) from the dead:

- the ruler's daughter (Matthew 9:18-25)

- the widow's son (Luke 7:12-15)

- Lazarus, brother of Mary and Martha (John 11:43-44)

During the Tribulation Period

Two servants of God will be raised from the dead (a mid-tribulation rapture), but they are yet future; these are the two witnesses raised during the time of The Great Tribulation (Revelation 11:11).

Enoch of the OT

Enoch, the seventh from Adam was not for God took him (Genesis 5:24). This was an OT rapture. It is not said of Enoch that he died or that he was raised from the dead before God took him to Heaven. Enoch's departure from earth to Heaven was a translation or rapture similar to that of the Church's future departure.

(**NOTE:** The eight mentioned above are *individuals* raised from the dead. There was also a large body of many saints [collectively] that arose out of their graves **after** Christ's resurrection and appeared in Jerusalem [Matthew 27:52, 53]. It is also worth mentioning that many Bible students believe that Jonah died in the whale and was raised to life again. Some also believe that Paul was stoned to death outside of Lystra, caught up to Paradise in Heaven, and finally raised from the dead. Of course, though it may be implied, the Bible does not expressly state that Jonah and Paul died.)

> *Matthew 27:52-53: And the graves were opened;* *and* ***many bodies of the saints which slept arose, And came out of the graves;*** *after his resurrection, and went into the holy city, and appeared unto many.*

-Notice that these were OT Saints that were resurrected "after" Christ's resurrection. It appears to the writer that these were the "firstfruits" of Christ's resurrection (I Corinthians 15:23).

Seeing as how only about ten individual souls in six-thousand years of history have been biblically reported as having been raised from the dead, the present claims of many people being raised from the dead by some charismatic preachers are silly and ludicrous.

Ludicrous Claim of Raising the Dead

This writer (March 2008) was told by a member of Living Branch Ministries (north of Greer, S C), of a South African evangelist who would be the guest speaker at his church on March 16-17, 2008. (The gentleman that relayed this story to the writer was a volunteer counselor and soul-winner with this writer at a charitable organization (Miracle Hill Ministries of Greenville, S. C.). The single-page handout flier concerning the ministry of this visiting evangelist stated, "God has worked through brother Surprise (Surprise "Supressa" Sithole) **to raise 50 deceased persons from the dead** and untold numbers have been healed of varying illnesses and diseases."

The flier goes on to say, "Mr. Sithole is welcomed with open arms and we are expecting exciting things to take place in the Spirit: The Anointing and Glory of God's presence will fall – signs – wonders and miracles will take place." When I asked my friend if the evangelist would be able to accompany me to a nursing home, he replied that Mr. Sithole was only one man and could not spare the time. He also said you have to bring them to Mr. Sithole. The writer wondered if there was a limitation upon the age of the dead corpse to qualify as being "raised from the dead," or if I had to take a dead corpse to Sithole.

Mr. Sithole did not raise anyone from the dead in my neighborhood. I have a copy of the flier in my files. Other charismatics have made similar false claims of raising the dead.

➢ **Has the reader ever heard about any modern *so-called* healer entering hospitals and nursing homes to set the infirmed free of their maladies?**

ANSWER: NO.

➢ **Has the reader even wondered why the alleged healers DO NOT?**

ANSWER: Hopefully the reader can reason this answer independently. The alleged healers 'shut up" because they will not "show up" and "put up."

The writer believes that a person endowed with miraculous healing power would take the initiative (without an invite) to visit hospitals and nursing homes with blessings of anointed miraculous healings. If this writer laid claim to healing power, he would spend some time at the hospital emergency rooms on Saturday nights. To date, the writer has received no offers from the healers to attend Shriner's Hospital or a nursing home. THE OFFER STILL STANDS. **Applicants may contact the writer at the address included at the end of this writing.**

➢ **Are Bodily Healings Provided for in the Atonement of Christ? Does I Peter 2:24 Justify Physical Healings?**

Answer: No for both questions.

> *I Peter 2:24: Who his own self bare our sins in his own body on the tree, that we, being dead to sins, should live unto righteousness: **by whose stripes ye were healed.***

As for the body, eventually all believers will receive a glorified body like the body of Christ at the believer's First Resurrection. The resurrection body is the only healing of the body that is guaranteed for the believer. All miraculously healed people will eventually die. There will be a body that will never become sick and in this sense, there is a guaranteed healing of the body. The healing in I Peter 2:24 is a healing of the soul and spirit, not the body. This can easily be seen by referring back to the book of Isaiah:

➢ **Isaiah 53:**

> *Surely he hath borne our griefs, and carried our sorrows: yet we did esteem him stricken, **smitten of God**, and afflicted.*

> *But he was wounded for our transgressions, he was bruised for our iniquities: the chastisement of our peace was upon him; **and with his stripes we are healed**.*

*All we like sheep have gone astray; we have turned every one to his own way; and **the LORD hath laid on him the iniquity of us all***.

*He was oppressed, and he was afflicted, yet he opened not his mouth: h**e is***

***brought as a lamb to the slaughter**, and as a sheep before her shearers is dumb,*

so he openeth not his mouth.

This is a prophecy of Messiah written hundreds of years before Jesus came into the world in a body of flesh and provided the final atonement (propitiation; reconciliation). Jesus came into the world in the form of a man (incarnate in a body of flesh) to die on Calvary's cross for sinful man (Luke 10:10). The OT saints of Isaiah chapter 53 were said to be spiritually healed by Hs stripes long before Christ's atonement (propitiation for our sins) was expressed in I Peter 2:24. The fact of OT saints healed by his stripes does not support the opinion that I Peter 2:24 is teaching that the healing of the body is provided for in the atonement of Christ. This healing of OT saints occurred before the atonement (propitiation; reconciliation). Of course, Jesus died on the cross for sinners of all ages, but that does not guarantee bodily healing upon request or demand. Of course, the of all saints will be totally healed when they receive their glorified bolies like unto the body of glorified Christ. Apostles Paul healed others and earnestly sought healing for himself but was to no avail. The Scripture of I Peter 2:24 is not speaking about physical healing (although miracles of healing attested to His divine authority and that of His apostles). If physical healings can be claimed and presumed to be had, where, when, and how is man's eventual death to be reckoned? It is appointed unto man once to die (Hebrews 9:27) and so man must expect his body to become ill to some measure in order to die. If Jesus had healed his own broken body, He could not have died for our sins. Are we too good to be sick or infirmed? Paul was not; Timothy was not; Stephen was not. Many others were not and neither are there any today that are too spiritual and beyond getting sick or infirmed.

These Scriptures speak bout God's provision of salvation (the spiritual healing of the soul). This is God's offering up of the perfect sacrifice for healing our wounds of sin, by His only begotten Son (John 3:16; Romans 5:19; I Corinthians 5:7; 15:3; Galatians 3:8; 4:4-5; 6:14; Colossians 1:20; I Timothy 1:15; Hebrews 2:9; 9:12, 26, 28; 10:12; 12:2; I Peter 2:24).

Our charismatic brethren instantly jump to the conclusion that we who disagree with their version of divine healing are denying God's willingness and power to heal. Of course, the God of Creation can heal in any dispensation but not according to the traditions of men. Since physical death is undeniable, the salvation of his soul is of primary importance. Jesus said that a man must be "born again" (John 3:3, 5, 7).

(**NOTE**: While visiting a patient at the Columbia, South Carolina Insane Asylum many years ago, the writer observed that there were some people dressed up and simply standing along roadsides within the institution property. The writer also noticed that none of them were ever picked up by any vehicle. These people were holding Bibles in their hands as if they were waiting to be presently picked up to attend church. When the writer inquired about this, employees of the institution told me that these people were not visitors but were non-violent inmates of that institution (*Unlike violent inmates, they had liberties of freely moving around*). The writer was further told that these inmates were of a religion that had demanded miraculous body healings that never happened. In their frustration, they had nervous breakdowns when they did not receive assumed answers to their prayer of faith (*They did not lack faith*). Since these inmates had not received answers to their prayers in a manner according to their understanding, they became mentally and emotionally disturbed to the point of having to be institutionalized. Although the writer admires their wonderful but misguided faith in miraculous healing, he also was sad concerning their misunderstanding of bodily healing. The writer was not surprised.)

Of course, the writer does not intend to imply in any way that we should not pray for healing. We need to accept the outcome of the prayer to be God's will in the matter. You cannot demand that God answer your prayer according to your will. The writer believes that prayer for healing should precede a visit to the doctor. To believe that God is compelled to heal when it is not His will to do so could certainly cause great emotional stress as these inmates were experiencing.

<u>Healing Instructions Given to the Early Jewish Christians</u>

> *James 1:1; 5:13-15: James, a servant of God and of the Lord Jesus Christ,* **to the twelve tribes** *which are scattered abroad, greeting. Is any among you afflicted?* **Let him pray.** *Is any merry? Let him sing psalms. Is any sick among you?* **Let him call for the elders of the church;** *and let them* **pray over him, anointing him with oil** *in the name of the Lord: And* **the prayer of faith** *shall save the sick, and the Lord shall raises him up; and* **if he have committed sins,** *they shall be forgiven him.*

(**NOTE:** Some Christians do not feel that *anointing with oil* is required for NT Christians while others prefer to use it. Oil was used as a sign of miraculous healing {Mark 6:13} and it was used afterwards by the elders of the early church [James 5:14]. There are also some that believe that this "prayer of faith" of James 5:15 may refer to a providential prompting by God Himself for His own glory rather than man's choosing of his own accord. Of course, the reader is free to determine these things for himself as the Spirit of God leads. Perhaps the text could be associated with **the probability of sin in the believer's life**, "…and **if** he have committed sins…".)

Why No Peace in the World

> *James 4:1-3: From whence come wars and fightings among you? Come they not hence, even of your lusts that war in your members? Ye lust, and have not: ye kill, and desire to have, and cannot obtain: ye fight and war, yet ye have not, because ye ask not. Ye ask, and receive not, because ye ask amiss, that ye may consume it upon your lusts.*

Bible prophecy reveals that *"wars and fightings"* will not cease until Jesus puts down all evil by Himself.

The real problem of the world is within the hearts of men, not in extraneous matters which are common to all men - I Corinthians 10:13.

*Genesis 6:5: And God saw that the wickedness of man was great in the earth, and that every imagination of the thoughts of his **heart** was only evil continually.*

*Proverbs 4:23: Keep thy **heart** with all diligence; for out of it are the issues of life.*

*Proverbs 16:9: A man's **heart** deviseth his way: but the LORD directeth his steps.*

*Proverbs 23:7: For as he thinketh in his **heart**, so is he.*

*Jeremiah 17:9: The **heart** is deceitful above all things, and desperately wicked: who can know it?*

*Matthew 12:34: For out of the abundance of the **heart** the mouth speaketh.*

Cure for the Wicked Heart

Isaiah 1:18: Come now, and let us reason together, saith the LORD: though your sins be as scarlet, they shall be as white as snow; though they be red like crimson, they shall be as wool.

Although this admonition is addressed to Israel, it also has a contemporary application to individuals of every age.

*Romans 10:9-10: That if thou shalt confess with thy mouth the Lord Jesus, and shalt believe in thine **heart** that God hath raised him from the dead, thou shalt be saved. For with the **heart** man believeth unto righteousness; and with the mouth confession is made unto salvation.*

Romans 10:13: For whosoever shall call upon the name of the Lord shall be saved.

Mark 8:38: Whosoever therefore shall be ashamed of me and of my Words in this adulterous and sinful generation; of him also shall the Son of man be ashamed, when he cometh in the glory of his Father with the holy angels.

Also refer to Luke 9:26; Romans 1:16; 9:33; 10:11; 2 Timothy 1:8, 12; Hebrews 2:11; 11:16; I Peter 4:16.

Does Prophecy Reveal to us the End of the World (Age) and the Order of Events?

ANSWER: Yes, prophecy tells us much about the "End of the Age" and what follows afterwards on earth.

There will be wars and rumors of wars in the end time. Wars are even now happening in many places of the world. However, there appears to be at least two major wars that will occur before Armageddon (Armageddon will occur near the end of The Great Tribulation Period). Major wars are listed in Psalms 83, Ezekiel chapters 38, 39, and Revelation 16:16).

The First Resurrection

I) The next major event of spiritual significance is the future prophecy of **The First Resurrection**. The First Resurrection is restricted to believers in Christ only. The dead in Christ (corrupted bodies of deceased believers) **rise first** (resurrected). The deceased have then put on incorruptible bodies. Afterwards, Christ **changes** the mortal bodies of living saints into immortal bodies. Both of these two companies of believers (the dead in Christ and the living saints) are the "main body" of The First Resurrection spoken of in Revelation 20. Together, both the incorruptible (resurrected dead) and immortal (changed living) are **caught up together** (raptured; caught up in clouds) to meet the Lord IN THE AIR- (See I Thessalonians 4:17; 5:9; I Corinthians 15:51-58. I Thessalonians 1:10; 4:13-18; Revelation 3:10; 4:1; Romans 5:9; Titus 2:13).

(**NOTE:** Notice that above, the writer mentioned the "main body" of the First Resurrection. The First Resurrection is likened to an agriculture harvest of which there are three parts: **Wave-Sheaf of the Firstfruits** [I Corinthians 15:20]; **Main Harvest**

[I Corinthians 15:51-58; I Thessalonians 4:13-18]; **Gleanings** [Revelation 7:14]).

THERE ARE SEVERAL RAPTURES OF BELIEVERS (Viz., OT Enoch; Elijah; NT believers; two witnesses of mid-tribulation; believers of post-tribulation; et al.)

The rapture, commonly referred to for the Church, (Bride or body of Christ) is the pre-millennial, pre-tribulation rapture/resurrection (I Corinthians 15:51-58; I Thessalonians 4:13-18).

The other major rapture is a pre-millennial, post-tribulation rapture/resurrection of tribulation saints (Revelation 7:9-14; 6:9-11).

The Tribulation Period

II.) Following the First Resurrection of the Church, a time called **The Tribulation Period** of seven years begins. This period is also called "The Time of Jacob's Trouble" (Jeremiah 30:7) and "Daniel's 70th Week of Prophecy" (Daniel 9:24-27). This is Jewish time.

A devil-man (called Antichrist in John's letters to the churches), who has great oratory skills and a charismatic personality, will appear on the international scene. The Antichrist will have a magnetic personality and will be energized and totally controlled by Satan himself. With his oratory skills, he will be a convincing figure to delude the world of his agenda by appearing to resolve earth's problems of the Jews. Antichrist will also satisfy the world concerning the mysterious disappearance of the Church. This satanic indwelt evil beast-man will have a seeming answer to the world's economic disaster and chronic wars among the nations. The false solutions of the Antichrist will sooth the ears of the troubled masses in the chaotic world.

Some think that the Antichrist personage will attribute the mass disappearance of earth dwellers (Christians called up in the First Resurrection/Rapture/Translation) to alien kidnappers from another world. To the secular mind, this may explain all the hoopla about UFO's and life on other planets?

All supernatural manifestations are either of God or demons, not "so called:' alien life-forms from other planets. Many allege that space aliens seeded earth with the first humans (called "transpermia"). These UFO sighting are alleged to be aliens from other planets returning to earth to assess the progress and development of their seeded "earth" children. The Vatican scientists are strong believers of this delusion.

Our government is foolishly spending billions of dollars of our tax money in an effort to find the origin of life in outer space. This is a great waste of time and money.

In the beginning, the parents of all human life were Adam, the first man and Eve, the mother of all living. Anyone denying this truth is guilty of making God's Word a lie. Adam and Eve together were the progenitors of all human life. Humanity began on planet earth, not in outer space. We read about it in many books of God's Word (Genesis; John; Ephesians; Colossians; etc.)

"...Awake thou that sleepest, and arise from the dead, and Christ shall give thee light" – *Ephesians 5:14.)*

On July 7, 2011, Pope Benedict XVI released an encyclical "Caritas in Veritate," or "Charity in Truth," calling for a New World Order (Exo-Vaticanus, p. 211). The pope is aiding in laying the groundwork for his successors (False Prophet) and the Antichrist.

The antichrist will assume to solve earth's greatest "alleged" problem, Israel, by confirming a 7-year Covenant with them (probably Israel forfeiting land for peace and safety). This covenant will probably be ratified by most of the nations of the world (Today, most of the nations are opposed to Israel). This will be Jewish time of a 7-Year Period which is the final 70th Week of Daniel's Prophecy (Daniel 9:24-27) and the Time of Jacob's Trouble (Jeremiah 30:7).

Through biblical prophecy, we know that Satan will indwell *that man of sin* in the Tribulation Period of the end time (2 Thessalonians 2:3; Revelation 13:1). Probably this "entering in" of the man of sin by Satan is analogous to when Satan entered into Judas Iscariot. Obviously, the possession of the man of sin (the antichrist personage) by Satan will be a "total" possession dictating Antichrist's every move (This is unlike people that are indwelt with demons but still have some power to execute their own will).

The last half (or, 3 ½ years) of the 7-year period is called "The Great Tribulation." In the middle of the 7-year time of Jacob's Trouble, the Antichrist will break his covenant with Israel and seek to destroy them; Antichrist will also set up his Abomination of Desolation in the rebuilt Temple and declare that all the world worship him as God.

Sometime within the 7-Year Tribulation Period, the beast out of the earth (Antichrist's right-hand man) will cause all, both small and great, rich and poor, free and bond, to receive a mark in their right hand, or in their foreheads (Revelation 13:11-16). No one will be allowed to buy or sell (transact any business) "...save he that had the mark, or the name of the beast, or the number of his name" (Revelation 13:17). Any person that receives the antichrist mark of the beast will seal their doom forever.

CHAPTER 12

MARK OF THE BEAST OF REVELATION 13

The writer does not believe that the doom of those who receive the mark of the beast during the Tribulation Period is attributable to simply receiving a mark or number. Receiving this mark has a much deeper, darker meaning. The writer believes that the true meaning of the reception of the beast-mark or number is a soul-damning acknowledgement of the man of sin as Messiah (John 5:43; 2 Thessalonians 2:10-12). The reception of the mark is a demonic acceptance of Satan's counterfeit Christ, Antichrist, as deity. The Bible calls this the Abomination of Desolation (Matthew 24:15, 23), a form of blasphemy that is counter-paralleled in the Gospels. For example, the unbelieving Jews attributed the "wonderful works" of Christ to demonic power (Matthew 12:28-32). This was considered blasphemy against the Holy Spirit and was never to be forgiven. In a dissimilar way the "wicked workings" of Antichrist and the demonic forces during the Tribulation Period are attributed to Messiah by those that accept the mark of the beast. The acceptance of the mark of the beast preserves the physical life of deluded souls a little longer but seals their future everlasting damnation (Revelation 14:9-11).

The writer believes that the mark of the beast will be some sort of electronic micro-chip implanted beneath or "in" the body ("...receive a mark **in** their right hand, or **in** their foreheads," not necessarily "on"). These chips are already a reality. They are presently designed to locate stray animals, stolen vehicles, and some say for victims of Alzheimer's disease. Of course, by the implantation of a microchip, a person's location can be tracked anywhere in the world that they might try and hide (Big Brother of 1984 is a little late coming).

The writer is impressed at the advancement of satellite technology. When he first turned on his GPS satellite navigator, it told him his address and pinpointed him on a street map; while traveling down the road, it told the writer his exact automobile speed while traveling down the interstate highway, it identified the highway that the writer was traveling upon as well as the intersecting highways that he was approaching before he even arrived at them (and the writer's navigator was not top-line technology). **The New World Order** technology is already in place for implementing by the Antichrist.

(**NOTE:** There is a mysterious monument outside of Elberton, GA dedicated to the   New World Order. On one of the highest hilltops in Elberton County, Georgia stands a   huge granite monument. The New Age monument is engraved in eight different   languages. On the four giant stones that support the common capstone, are 10 guides,   or commandments. This monument is alternately referred to as The Georgia Guidestones, or the American Stonehenge. Though relatively unknown to most people, it is an important link to the Occult Hierarchy that dominates the world in which we live. The origin of that strange monument is shrouded in mystery because no one knows the true identity of the man, or men, who commissioned its construction. The writer viewed this Babylonian New Age Shrine in 2007.)

The Number 666

The number 666 is the number of the beast of Revelation 13. The number "7" is the number of completion or finality. After God's creation, He rested on the seventh day. The number **"6" is man's number.** **Man** was created on the sixth day of creation. The final disposition of **evil man** is seen in the number "666." We can see three 6's of the 666 materialize in the unholy trinity of the devil, the beast, and the false prophet (Revelation 20:10; 19:20; 13:1, 11, 13, 14, 16, 18). The writer thought it was interesting that the sixth word of the sixth verse of the sixth chapter of the sixth book of the New Testament would be the word "man." (Romans 6:6).

Blasphemous Imitation by Satan

In imitation of the Holy Trinity or "Tri-Unity" of the Godhead (Father; Son; Holy Ghost), Satan emulates God in an "unholy trinity" (dragon/devil, beast, and false prophet – Revelation 16:13; 19:20; 20:10). Satan attempts to damn souls of men by cleverly imitating the salvation of man by "a way that seemeth right unto a man" (Proverbs 14:12; 16:25), but it is a false way (John 14:6). Jesus alone is the true way and Satan tries to supplant God's truth with clever lying imitations (false ways). In Revelation 17, we see the religious whore (Babylon) riding upon the back of the One-World Political Antichrist System. There has only been **one** phony *religion* since the time of Christ that has controlled world governments for centuries and also slain millions of Christians under the color of law. This apostate system operated under the guise (or, "cover") of religion that pretends to follow Christ. True martyrs for Jesus were falsely branded as heretics by the phony state religion. This false religious system probably heads up the final apostate world religion which is symbolized by "Babylon" (Revelation chapters 17, 18). Perhaps the reader should read Foxes Book of Martyrs, Trail of the Blood, and Baptist History.

(**NOTE**: It is not clear to this writer as to **when** [before or after the rapture] that the nations listed in Ezekiel's prophecy will attack Israel and subsequently be destroyed by God. The nations are listed in Ezekiel 38-39. These nations are identified by many scholars as:: Rosh [Russia]; Persia [modern-day Iran]; Turkey; Armenia; Gomer [Germany]; Libya and Ethiopia [parts of Africa]; Missing in this list is Iraq.)

In the middle of Daniel's 70th Week of Prophecy, or 3 ½ years from the beginning of the 7-Year Covenant, the antichrist will break his covenant with the Jews:

> *Daniel 9:27: "And he* (antichrist) *shall confirm the covenant with many* (Israel and the Gentile nations) *for one week* (7 years): *and **in the midst of the week*** (3 ½ Years), *he shall cause the sacrifice and the oblation to cease..."*

Satan will also energize the false prophet of Revelation 13:11-14; 16:13; 19:20; 20:10. With the help of the false prophet (satanic world religious leader) and his miracles, Satan, acting in the person of Antichrist, will seize control of the nations of the world by using **a three-point attack.** This assault will be realized in the pagan Babylonian Revival within the Old Roman Empire in the form of **Political Babylon** (dictatorial World-Wide Government), **Religious Babylon** (The Global Harlot Church of Revelation 17), and **Commercial Babylon** (Global control of all business, economics, buying, selling, trade, etc.

Political Babylon

a.) **Political Babylon (Revelation 13:1-2; 17:12-13):** The United Nations, the EU (European Union), or some other organization, will be instrumental in the formation of Political Babylon which will be headed up by the antichrist personage. Other nations will be subordinate to the 10 ruling nations (10 toes of Daniel's Beast) that will be ruled by Antichrist. There is now a push to enact a global tax through the United Nations upon the nations and our current Muslim president (Hussein Obama) is pushing this agenda.

There are those prophecy writers (Viz., J. R. Church; Logsdon) that believe that America may be "political Babylon" and some give convincing arguments to substantiate this claim. The writer has not ruled out this possibility.

Ecclesiastical Babylon

b.) **Ecclesiastical Babylon (Revelation 17:1-7):** An amalgamation of The World

Council of Churches, the Ecumenical Movement (a blend of Charismatics, apostate Baptists, Pentecostals, and Protestants), the major cults (Catholicism, Islam, Buddhism, Taoism, Hinduism, Shintoism, etc.), and all of the minor cults and sects (Jehovah Witness; Mormon; etc.).

This religious whore will be headed up by the "Beast out of the Earth" (the false prophet) of Revelation 13:11 who causes the earth and them that dwell therein to worship the "Beast out of the Sea" (Revelation 13:1, 12). This religious harlot will be destroyed by Political Babylon (Revelation 17:16-18; 18).

(**NOTE:** Rome claims to be Babylon [undoubtedly religious Rome] according to the Roman Catholic Bible, *Confraternity Edition of The New Testament*, N.Y., 1963, p. 337.)

Will the pope be the antichrist as many Reformation Protestants believed?

The writer does not believe that the pope will be the antichrist personage, but he does believe that he is the most promising candidate for the **"False Prophet"** (beast out of the earth). See Revelation 13:11-14; 16:13; 19:20; 20:10. The beast out of the earth is the leader of this global religious system that is called **MYSTERY BABYLON THE GREAT, THE MOTHER OF HARLOTS AND ABOMINATIONS OF THE EARTH** (Revelation 17:5). The **apostate** religionists will be in subjection to the pope. The beast out of the earth (false prophet) will be subordinate (Revelation 13:12) to the beast out of the sea (Antichrist) who arises out of the sea (people or nations (Revelation 13:1-2). Of course, the Antichrist will be completely subordinate to Satan. The harlot church is not a true church and she is **the mother of all harlot churches**. The Unholy Trinity is composed of Satan, Antichrist, and the False Prophet.

Commercial Babylon

c.) **Commercial Babylon (Revelation 18:9-19; 13:17):** This could be in reference to the literal country of Babylon. The capital of the commercial Babylon may not be Baghdad or the *city or town* of OT Babylon, which was in the *country* of Babylon. The original "country" of Babylon included more than just the capital city Babylon and the present country of Iraq. The original country of Babylon also contained parts of other present day middle-east countries. The geographical headquarters of the Babylon of chapter

18 of the book of Revelation *could be* Dubai or located in Dubai, United Arab Emirates, the New Babylon, **not** New York, the Vatican, or Rome, as some commentators suggest.

(The United Arab Emirates [UAE] is a federation of seven independent states located in the SE corner of the Arabian Peninsula. It is bordered by the Persian Gulf to the north, Saudi Arabia to the south and west, and Oman and the Gulf of Oman to the east. The seven member states are Abu Dhabi [Abu Zaby], Ajman, Dubai, Al Fujayrah, Ra's al Khaymah, Ash Sharigah, and Umm al Qaywayn. The city of Abu Dhabi, located in the emirate of the same name, is the federal capital and the largest city. The federation is roughly crescent-shaped. The UAE's proven oil reserves make up almost one-tenth of the world's total.)

There is also a strong belief among Bible students that American fits the description of commercial Babylon of the end times.

It appears that the European Trade Nations will rule over their eastern and western counterparts. The antichrist personage will rule the commercial world (buying and selling) through these 10 toes of Daniel's beast, which are 10 leading nations. Perhaps the European Common Market is the prototype. No man might buy or sell save he that has the mark of the beast (Revelation 13:17). Commercial Babylon weeps over the destruction of Religious Babylon when Political Babylon destroys it (Revelation 18:11-19).

These three forms of the Revived Roman Empire or European Union (warmed over idolatry with vestiges of the pagan empires of Babylon, Medo-Persia, and Greece) are the big players in the last one-world antichrist system of government. Study chapters 13, 17, and 18 of the book of Revelation. The Bible lists four Gentile World Empires, Babylon, Medo-Persia, Greece, and Rome in Daniel's prophecy (Daniel 2:37-40; 7:1-7; 8:20-26). In John's prophecy, we see a composite beast of those ancient empires. For a brief time in history, Satan and his counterparts, the beast and the false prophet, will rule a Fifth World Empire,

> (Note: The ancient empires of Assyria and Egypt are omitted in Daniel's prophecy but are included in the Kingdom Age (Isaiah 19:23-25).

Actually, the empires of Babylon, Medo-Persia, Greece, and Rome were prophesied (Daniel chapters 2, 7, & 8). Hitler (probably the killer of more Jews than any single person) came close to creating a 5th World Empire. Again, the Antichrist will be the 5th short-lived, last evil-empire world ruler. The writer calls the wicked antagonists of Israel the 3-H devils, Haman, Herod, and Hitler.

The writer believes that a great economic situation (shortage of food and water) will grip the world. It also appears from signs of the times that eventually the USA will devolve into such an economic morass that an Amero-dollar or an International Currency Unit (ICU) will eventually be issued, perhaps just before or at the beginning of the 7-Years Tribulation Period.

During the Great Tribulation (the last 3 ½ Years of the 7-Year Tribulation Period), the most horrendous judgments ever known to man will be poured out upon earth dwellers which will be a time of judgments upon the Gentile nations as well as the purging of the nation of Israel. The end-time of The Great Tribulation is synonymous with the end of the age.

III.) (see the previous chapter for I and II) At the end of Daniel's 70th Week of Prophecy (The 7-Year Tribulation Period; The Time of Jacob's Trouble), Christ returns to earth (The Second Advent) **with** ten thousands of his saints to earth to execute judgment (Jude 14-15; Revelation 19:11, 15). At this time, **the beast out of the sea** (antichrist – Revelation 13:1, 4, 8, 12) and **the beast out of the earth** (false prophet – Revelation 13:11-15), that wrought miracles before the antichrist, will be cast alive into a lake of fire burning with brimstone (Revelation 19:20).

IV.) After Jesus destroys the remnant of his enemies (Revelation 19:21; Jude 15), He establishes the Throne of David in Jerusalem and He Himself reigns for a thousand years. At this time, the sin curse upon man and earth is removed. Also, that old serpent, which is the Devil, and Satan, is bound for a thousand years (Revelation 20:2-3).

V.) At the end of Christ's Thousand-Year-Reign upon the earth, Satan will be loosed out of his prison and shall go out to gather the nations together to battle...and fire came down from heaven and devoured them (Revelation. 20:7-9). The devil will be defeated and cast into the lake of fire and brimstone, where the beast and the false prophet are, and shall be tormented day and night for ever and ever (Revelation 20:7-10).

VI.) After the final disposition of Satan into the lake of fire and brimstone, where the beast and the false prophet were, **The Great White Throne Judgment** occurs (Revelation 20:11-15). This judgment throne is for the dead only (unsaved sinners). All lost souls (those not found in the book of life) will be cast into the lake of fire. This is the **second death** (Revelation 20:11-15).

VII.) After the White Throne Judgment and in contrast to the earth's baptism with water of Noah's flood, the earth will receive a baptism of fire. Fire speaks of judgment and/or purging:

> *2 Peter 3:10: But the day of the Lord will come as a thief in the night; in the which the heavens shall pass away with a great noise, and **the elements shall melt with fervent heat**, the earth also and the works that are therein shall be burned up.*

The base and simplest form of any substance is an "element." Many elements have been discovered and are listed in "The Periodic Chart of the Elements."

VIII.) After the earth's purging or baptism with fire, we have a New World, a New Heaven, a New Earth, and a New Jerusalem (Revelation 21:1-2). The Perfect Eternal Age now begins. Some prefer to call this age an 8th dispensation of a new beginning.

The writer has listed the future coming events in their probable chronological order (without attempting to fill in all of the gaps and details). The details are many and nearly every day meaningful prophetical events are occurring.

For the child of God, this is the end of tears, death, sorrow, crying, and pain. All of these have passed away:

*Revelation 21:4: And God shall wipe away all **tears** from their eyes: and there shall be no more **death**, neither **sorrow**, nor **crying**, neither shall there be any more **pain**; for the former things are passed away.*

The Scriptures are plain about the End-Time. Isaiah's voice of prophecy says:

Isaiah 40:4: Every valley shall be exalted, and every mountain and hill shall be made low: and the crooked shall be made straight, and the rough places plain.

Of course, all of the schemes of man are "hopeless humanism." Unless man allows God to change his heart, he will never achieve any successful degree of peace with himself or his fellowman.

In the book of Second Peter, **Prophecy is** to this world as a light in a dark place... Even as Venus, a morning star, is to the dark till the day dawns:

*2 Peter 1:18-19: And **this voice** which came from heaven we heard, when we were with him in the holy mount. We have **a more sure word of prophecy**; whereunto ye do well that ye take heed, **as unto a light** that shineth in a dark place, until the day dawn, and **the day star** (Christ) arise in your hearts.*

The Holy Spirit, speaking through Peter, says that the Old Testament **Bible prophecies were more sure than a**

supernatural voice from heaven (2 Peter 1:18). Bible prophecies are more sure and certain to us than a light in a dark place and Venus in the morning. We have seen the historical fulfillment of prophecies. Of course, the prophecy came not in old time by the will of man: but holy men of God spake as they were moved by the Holy Ghost (2 Peter 1:21).

The Word of God (Moses and the prophets) is more powerful to persuade than even miracles themselves (Luke 16:31).

CHAPTER 13

POPULARLY TOUTED PROPHECIES

Popularly Touted Prophecies of Secular Sources Not Reliable

Some are deceived by false prophets of latter times that are **not** of God. It amazes this writer that unbelievers will cling to a single lucky prophecy (or demon assisted one) that appears to have a grain of truth. These same people completely ignore numerous *failed* prophecies by the same false prophets. A true Bible prophet never missed a single prophecy or any detail of his prophecy. Again, the writer would remind the reader that even a blind hog might occasionally root up an acorn. *A word to the wise is sufficient.*

Actually, based upon **the study of Scriptures**, this lowly writer himself has prophesied a few things that have come true. The writer's predictions were **not a revelation** given directly from God but simply **illumination** of the Scriptures by the Holy Spirit (2 Timothy 2:15; John 16:13; I Corinthians 2:13-16). The writer makes no claim to any degree of piety for he **knows** that he is of the least in the kingdom of God.

<u>Reliable Prophecy examples:</u>

- <u>The Tearing-Down Of The Berlin Wall</u>

The writer came to this conclusion in the late 1960's after studying the book of Ezekiel. Ezekiel 38:1-6: And the word of the LORD came unto me, saying, Son of man, set thy face against Gog (**prince**), the land of Magog (**land of Gog**), the chief (**"rosh" or Russia**) prince of Meshech (**Moscow**) and Tubal (**Tobolsk**), and prophesy against him, And say, Thus saith the Lord GOD; Behold, I am against thee, O Gog, the chief prince of Meshech and Tubal: And I will turn thee back, and put hooks into thy jaws, and I will bring thee forth, and all thine army, horses and horsemen, all of them clothed with all sorts of armour, even a great company with bucklers and shields, all of them handling swords: Persia (*Iran*), Ethiopia (*parts of Africa*), and Libya with them; all of them with shield and helmet: <u>Gomer (*Germany*), and all his bands</u>; the house of Togarmah (*Turkey/Armenia*) of the north quarter, and all his bands: and many people with thee.

This Bible passage is a description of a latter day invasion of Israel by Russia and her hordes (mostly Muslims). There appears to be only three periods of time when this Russian-led invasion could occur: a) Immediately before the beginning of The 7-year Tribulation Period (Daniel's 70th Week of Prophecy; The Time of Jacob's Trouble); b) Immediately after the beginning of 7-year Tribulation Period; 3); In the middle of the 7-Year Tribulation Period. The text above has a reference to "Gomer (Germany) and all his bands." The writer was aware that Germany was once divided and afterwards reunified by Bismarck in 1871. The Cold War after Germany's loss of two World Wars resulted in Berlin's split into east and west by the Berlin Wall (1961-1989). The writer reasoned that Germany must be re-unifed the second time in order to fulfill Ezekiel 38. Gomer with "all his bands" alludes to unification, not division. In order to be reunified, the Berlin Wall would have to come down. The writer advocated the fall of the Berlin Wall and Germany's reunification (1990) twenty years before President Reagan issued his bold challenge to the Russian president, "Mr. Gorbachev, tear down this wall."

Noteworthy is the identification of primitive Russia in the Ezekiel 38 passage by The *Scofield Reference Bible* (**Copyright 1909**) even before Russia began to become a prominent nation in **1917**.)

- <u>Catastrophe in America</u>

Zechariah 12:3: And in that day will I make **Jerusalem a burdensome stone for all people**: all that burden themselves with it shall be cut in pieces, though all the people of the earth be gathered together against it.

Based upon Zechariah's prophecy, (and other Bible references) and because America has been the chief supporter of modern Israel, the writer expected that evil forces would be directed against both nations. The writer has long suspected that the posterity of Ishmael and Esau (radical Muslim Palestinians) would play an important role in latter times. It was prophesied that the Ishmael's hand would be against every man.

> *Genesis 16:11-12: And the angel of the Lord said unto her, Behold, thou art with child, and shalt bear a son, and shalt call his name* **Ishmael**; *because the LORD hath heard thy affliction. And* **he will be a wild man: his hand will be against every man**, *and every man's hand against him; and he shall dwell in the presence of all his brethren.*

Anticipation of God's Judgment on America

Because God punished His national people Israel, the writer also anticipated God's judgment on America because of her pagan ways. Euphemisms in America abound:

♦ America justifies the annual slaughter of about 1.2-1.4 million babies by calling it a **"woman's choice"** or the hypocritical title of **"Planned Parenthood."** The so-called "butcher shops" that are designed for the murder of innocent babies are even called **"Women's Clinics."** Again, clinics are for healing, not murder. This carnage against innocent babies is a strike against the very image of God and His creation.

At the time of this initial writing, over 40 million babies have been murdered (aborted) since Roe vs. Wade in 1973. (Update: over 60 million abortions to 2015.)

♦ Sodomy has found fertile soil in "so called" Christian America. Sodomy was the prevalent sin of Sodom and Gomorrah before their destruction. Sodomy was the prominent sin before Noah's flood. Sodomy is tolerated under the misnomer euphemisms of "gay rights," "alternate lifestyle," or "domestic partners." One report in 2009 says that five states in America have legalized sodomite marriage.

◆ Sexual immorality is termed an issue of "freedom." Supporters of "therapeutic cloning" are now calling their procedure "nuclear transplantation" in an effort to change how people perceive the process.

◆ Over half of the people killed on our highways involve the use of alcohol (estimated at **over** 10,000 annually). Of course, drunkenness (euphemism: "alcoholicism") and the sin addiction is called a "disease." It is absolutely stupid to award the sin of drunkenness an honorable name by calling it a disease (disease is caused by germs, not by liquor which kills germs). Giving drunkenness a favorable label such as the euphemism alcoholism (to soften) does not erase it as a sin condemned by the Bible. According to a panel convened by The National Institutes of Health last year (2000).

◆ America is experiencing an epidemic of STD's (sexually transmitted diseases). Sixty percent of co-eds at Rutgers University were found to be infected with HPV at some time during a three-year study. A study of herpes infection showed that 45.9 percent of all African-Americans over the age of 11 in this country are infected. There has been a 500 percent increase in the prevalence of genital herpes in white adolescents over the past 25 years - *(To Tell the Truth about Condoms*, Joe S. McIlhaney, Jr., M.D., *The Times Examiner*, page 10, dated November 7, 2001).

◆ We also exhibited the depth (or shallowness) of our nation's "so called" Christian heritage when a single professing atheist was able to take prayer and Bible reading out of public schools and government agencies (on the pretext of separation of church and state). Carried to its logical end, this would eliminate any genuine Christian from serving in government.

◆ It is very common today for people to be labeled as "fiancées" who have lived together for several years and have children.

Neither was the writer greatly surprised at Hurricanes Andrew (FL) and Hugo (SC & NC)

◆ Tornadoes (all over the nation)

◆ Floods (The Great Mississippi River & others)

◆ Earthquakes, fires, and mudslides

◆ Fires (western states and even sub-tropical Florida)

◆ Volcano eruption (Mt. St. Helens)

Spree Killers, Mass Murderers, and Serial Killers of America

◆ **Spree Killers, Mass Murderers, and Serial Killers of America:** Spinks; Charles Starkweather; Charles Whitman; Paul John Knowles; Eliot & Gilbert; Ted Bundy; John Wayne Gacy; Jeffrey Dahmer; the Boston Strangler; Kenneth Bianchi & Angelo Buono (the Hillside Stranglers); Richard Ramirez (The Nightstalker); Brinkley; Joseph Christopher; the Zodiac Killer; Stayner; Wainright; James Cubaddage; Charles Albright; Caesar Baroni; Timothy Spencer; Herb Baumeister; Larry Gene Bell; Arthur Shawiwiss; Joel Rifkin; Robert Silveria (The Boxcar Killer); Charles Manson (Sharon Tate murders); Christopher Wilder (The Model Killer); Ted Kaczynski (The Unabomber); Cleopas Prince (Clairmont Killer); Jack Sully; Darren Dee O'Neall; William Sutt; Timothy McVeigh (Oklahoma Federal Building bombing); Miguel Colon (Alphabet Killer); Edmund Kemper (Santa Cruz co-ed murders); Gary Leon Ridgway (Green River Killer?); Daniel Conahan (Hog Trail Murderer); Danny Rolling (Gainesville, FL murders); Dana Sue Gray (female serial killer); Aileen Carol Wuornos (Florida's female serial killer); Glen Rogers; David Carpenter (Trailside Killer); Larry Eyler (Interstate Killer); Blanche Moore (The Black Widow Killer); Orville Majors (potassium chloride killer); Kenneth McDuff (Broomstick Killer); Michael Ronning; Barbara Stager; Bobby Joe Long; Dr. Michael Swango; James Randall; Colin Ferguson; Andrew Cunanan; Richard Grissom; the Briley brothers (James and Linwood); Roy and

Faye Copeland (Missouri Cattle Auctions Check Fraud Scam); James Perry and Lawrence Horn (contract murders of Silver Springs, MD); John Emil List (killed his entire family—mother, wife, and three children); Paul Bernardo; David Allen Lucas; Jeffrey Matthews; Dorothea Puente (Boarding House Murders); Faryion Wardrip; Efren Saldivar; Wayne Williams (Atlanta Child Murders); The I-45 Killer; Genene Jones; Steve Pennell (Corridor Killer); James Koedatich; Leonard Lake and Charles Ng (torture murders); Robert Lee Yates Jr. (Spokane murders and others); Juan Luna and James Degorski (killed 7 people at a fried chicken restaurant); Arthur Shawcross; Anthony John Sully; Dennis Rader, the BTK (**B**eat, **T**orture, and **K**ill) killer; David Berkowitz, the Son of Sam (killer of six people; many others suffered for a lifetime at his hand; sentenced to 365 consecutive years in 1978. It has been reported that he was converted to Christ after 10 years in prison). The list continues to grow.

(**NOTE:** According to the FBI report of 2002, there are fifty {50} serial killers at large in America.)

◆ Children killing parents (**euthanasia)** and parents killing children (**abortion**)

◆ Contemporary insurgence of fatalistic cults such as Branch Davidian, Jim Jones, Islamic Jihad, Heaven's Gate, etc.

◆ Terrorist attacks (around the world as well as at home in America (World Trade Center; Oklahoma Federal Bldg)

"Cashless Society

A "cashless society" is imminently approaching us. We are inundated with plastic credit cards, banking cards, debit cards, telephone cards, purchasing cards (vending machines, gas pumps, groceries, etc.) and electronic banking. In the future, it will be mandatory for social security retirees to "direct deposit" their retirement checks. Its just a matter of time until there will be introduced an "international currency unit" or ICU, similar to Europe's Euro currency or ECU (European Currency Unit).

The Times Examiner (Greenville, SC) edition of 10/30/02 reported that the FDA (Food and Drug Administration) quietly and suddenly notified the manufacturer of the Vera-Chip that their controversial micro-chip is approved for use in humans. The ID chips are approved for security, financial, personal identification and safety purposes but not for medical applications. The small transmitters, said to be slightly larger than a grain of rice, emits a radio frequency that may be picked up by a scanner up to 4 feet away. The chips have been used in animals in California for almost a year. Of course, there are good reasons that will justify the implanted chips such as speedily retrieving medical data of unconscious patients when the medical history is not otherwise available; and the ability to locate lost children; etc. Bible scholars and students see them as a possible forerunner of the "mark of the beast" mentioned in Bible prophecy. Critics are concerned that the requirement of such chips could be used as a control mechanism by pimps, gang leaders and governments (Shades of '1984's *Big Brother"*).

The writer envisions catastrophes to be perpetrated upon America of such a frightening nature that he will not even name them. The writer is aware that he may be considered an unpatriotic, hard-nose religionist (Jeremiah was persecuted for telling the truth) but he predicts that there will be no "national" revival of *true* religion in America. The writer prefers to be wrong. Perhaps there will be local revivals. However, the writer does predict extensive growth in false religion of two kinds, the cold, formalistic type (no fire) and the ecumenical charismatic kind (wild fire). Judgments upon America, by nature, Satan's cohorts, and America's enemies, will intensify. SIGNS OF THE TIMES!

Eye Contact with Big Brother

According to one report, many people have wondered about the television switchover from analog to digital and the little converter boxes that the government is helping people to purchase. It is quite a scheme, and the "upgrade" is one that will facilitate high-tech mind control. Our U.S. Military has used such technology for over ten years, and it was used on the Iraquis to bring them to their knees quickly when invaded in 1990. The technology is called *Silent Sound Spread Spectrum* or SSSS. U.S. Patent number 4,858,612 was issued to Philip Stocklin on December 19th, 1983, for the invention. It is also known as *sound of silence* (remember the Simon and Garfunkel song), and it works by transmission of sound undetected by the ear but planted into the human auditory cortex of the brain. It is the ultimate in universal mind control. If this system were attempted to be used with the old analog television, it would show up only as static. That is why everything must be converted to digital, and the government will help you pay for it. Don't put it past big brother to try to put the will of the Antichrist directly into your brain as you make eye contact with your digital television. You may find yourself thinking things you otherwise would never think and doing things you would otherwise never do! Incidentally, the first verse of the satanically prophetic song "The Sound of Silence: reads as follows*: "Hello darkness my old friend, I've come to talk with you again, Because a vision softly creeping, Left its seeds while I was sleeping, And the vision **that** was **planted in my brain** still remains, Within the sound of silence." /Last Trumpet Ministries/*

The writer does not know the degree of truth to this report but is not surprised at its claim. Also, the writer never thought he would live to see "so called" Christian religions endorse sodomy life-styles and its acceptance even in the pastorate (PCUSA; UMC; Anglican/Episcopal; Lutheran; United Church of Christ). Even the worst kind of sinner can easily see through this incredible charade of licentious pagan religion.

Is there a Bible Prophesy of a Translation or Rapture of True Believers

Is there a Bible Prophesy of a Translation or Rapture of True Believers Before the Great Tribulation?

ANSWER: Yes. The rapture or translation is the same as The First Resurrection.

A popular axiom says, "No one will get out of this world alive." The answer to that axiom is both true and false.

All true Christians (not professing Christians) that are living when Christ comes for His Bride (the Church) will be **changed** and **caught up** in clouds (raptured) to meet the Lord in the air. These saints will not experience a natural death.

> *I Corinthians 15:51-55: Behold, I shew you a mystery; We shall not all sleep* (die in Christ), *but **we shall all be changed**, In a moment, in the twinkling of an eye, at the last trump: for the trumpet shall sound, and the dead shall be raised incorruptible, and **we** (which are alive) **shall be changed**. For this corruptible* (body of dead believers) *must put on incorruption, and **this mortal** (body of living believers) **must put on immortality**. So when this corruptible shall have put on incorruption, and **this mortal shall have put on immortality**, then shall be brought to pass the saying that is written, **Death is swallowed up in victory**. **O death**, where is thy sting? **O grave** (death), **where is thy victory?***

This text clearly states that **all** living believers will be changed and escape death at the First Resurrection. Of course, the "all" militates against the "partial rapture theory."

> *I Thessalonians 4:13-17: But I would not have you to be ignorant, brethren, concerning them which are asleep, that ye sorrow not, even as other which have no hope. For if we believe that Jesus died and rose again, even so them also which sleep in Jesus will God bring with him. For this we say unto you by the word of the Lord, that **we which are alive and remain** unto the coming of the Lord shall not prevent (go before or precede) them which are asleep. **For the Lord himself shall descend from heaven** with a shout, with*

> *the voice of the archangel, and with the trump of God: and the dead in Christ shall rise first: Then* ***we which are alive and remain shall be caught up*** *together with them in the clouds,* ***to meet the Lord in the air****, and so shall be ever be with the Lord.*

-The Scriptures mean what they say and say what they mean. In these two texts, Christ comes **for** His saints who are caught up to meet Him in the air and then on to Heaven. In Christ's Second Advent, which is different from Christ coming **for** His saints, He comes to earth **with** ten thousands of His saints (Jude 14). If we do not heed the truth of Scriptures, we may remain ignorant (un-informed) and sorrowful concerning the resurrection of the dead and the translation of the living.

Believers are admonished to look for The Coming of Christ, not Antichrist:

> *I Thessalonians 1:10: And to* ***wait for his Son from heaven****, whom he raised from the dead, even Jesus, which* <u>delivered us from the wrath to come</u>*.*

> *Titus 2:13: Looking for that blessed hope, and the glorious appearing of the great God and our Saviour Jesus Christ.*

We are not admonished to look for Antichrist and the Great Tribulation but for the appearing of our Lord and Saviour. Believers are not appointed to wrath. (Romans 5:9; I Thessalonians 5:9; Revelation 3:10).

Left Behind

Lost people will not be included in The First Resurrection (translation of the Church). Unsaved "religious" sinners, along with unsaved non-religious sinners, will be "left behind" to endure a "Global Holocaust" and many will die horrible deaths during the *The Great Tribulation*. Although a great multitude of souls will be saved during the Great Tribulation (Revelation 7:9-14), it is certainly appears that **only those who had not heard** a clear presentation of *the Gospel of Christ*, before the Tribulation Period began, will have an opportunity to be saved. There were those that had heard the Gospel truth but "...received not the love of the truth, that they might be saved..."

> *2 Thessalonians 2:8-12: And then shall that Wicked be revealed, whom the Lord shall consume with the Spirit of his mouth, and shall destroy with the brightness of his coming: Even him, whose coming is after the working of Satan with all power and signs and lying wonders,* ***And with all deceivableness of unrighteousness in them that perish; because they received not the love of the truth****, that they might be saved. And for this cause* **God shall send them strong delusion,** *that they should believe a (the) lie:* ***That they all might be damned who believed not the truth*** *but had pleasure in unrighteousness*

False Hope

The popularly touted book "Left Behind" may give a false hope of a second chance for salvation for those enter into the Tribulation Period who have had a clear presentation of the Gospel and rejected it. The 2 Thessalonian passage above expressly states that those that loved **not** the truth (they had the truth before) shall be sent strong delusion that they all might be damned. Obviously, these that are condemned had the privilege of hearing and understanding, and yet, rejected the love of the Gospel of Jesus Christ beforehand. These will never again have an opportunity for salvation because God will send them strong delusion and they will believe the lie(s) of the Antichrist. This false hope for a chance of salvation is similar to Romans Catholicism's false dogma of a non-existent purgatory (middle ground; limbo state) that allows a second chance for salvation. This writer cannot find any such justification for establishing a "second chance" doctrine for those once enlightened but having rejected the Gospel truth. There is no more sacrifice for them.

In order to be saved during the Tribulation Period, believers will have to refuse the mark of the beast and many will be killed (Revelation 13:15-17). Beheading by the **guillotine** or **sword** (Revelation 20:4**)** will likely be the principal method of execution for those who refuse the beast's mark, his name, or his number during the Great Tribulation (The sword is the Muslim's favorite means of decapitating non-Muslims and non-conformers). If people in contemporary times (before The Tribulation Period) have heard the clear presentation of the Gospel and have refused to believe in Jesus Christ in times of which there is little or no persecution, it is quite certain that they will not accept the Lord under times of great duress and upon the threat of death. Again, many people refusing the mark, or the name of the beast, or the number of his name of the beast will be **beheaded** (Revelation 13:15-17; 20:4).

(**NOTE**: It should never be forgotten that there are many countries even today where true Christians suffer much persecution and even horrible deaths. Every Christian should read Fox's Book of Martyrs.)

The Lord promises those that believe and endure to the end (refuse the mark of the beast and endure the harsh persecution of the Gentile World System) during The Great Tribulation, will be saved (physical lives) at His coming (Matthew 10:22; 24:13).

Born Again Believers will be Changed

Before the 7-years Tribulation Period Begins, Born Again Believers will be Changed and Caught up in Clouds without Experiencing Death.

The translation of the living saints is commonly referred to as "The Rapture of the Church." The writer prefers to use "changed" or "translated" and "caught up" rather than the rapture term. This translation of the Church is synonymous with the main part of The First Resurrection. The First Resurrection is in three parts: 1) Christ and the First Fruits; 2) They that are His at His coming [the translation; rapture]; 3) The Tribulation saints [gleaning of the First Resurrection]. All true Christians (not mere "professing" Christians) that are living when Christ comes in the heavens will be **changed** and **caught up** in clouds to meet the Lord **in the air**. These saints will not experience death (at least, not in the natural sense).

Of course, the "dead in Christ" will rise first and both dead and living will be caught up together in clouds in the air to meet the Lord.

Again, present-day believers are not appointed to wrath (Romans 5:9; I Thessalonians 5:9; Revelation 3:10; Titus 2:13).

There are various interpretations concerning the translation of the Church. Because the various theories are commonly referred to as *Rapture Theories* and for the sake of clarity, the writer will use the term "rapture" instead of "translation" to define the various beliefs.

CHAPTER 14

BELIEFS IN CHRISTENDOM CONCERNING THE "RAPTURE"

Beliefs in Christendom Concerning the "Translation" and "Catching Up" of "Living Believers"

In Christendom, there are several views concerning the translation (rapture) of the church. <u>Following are the most prominent teachings</u>:

Pre-Millennial Pre-Tribulation Rapture

1.) **Pre-Millennial Pre-Tribulation Rapture:** This group believes that all living believers (Church; Body of Christ) will be changed and caught up in clouds (raptured) to meet the Lord in the air before the Millennium and also before the 7-Tear Tribulation Period. The 7-Year Tribulation Period is Jewish time and the last week of Daniel's 70 Weeks of Prophecy concerning Israel (Daniel 9:24-27). The true Church, which is Christ's body, is not part of Jewish time.

Pre-Millennial Mid-Tribulation Rapture

2.) **Pre-Millennial Mid-Tribulation Rapture:** This group believes that the Church will be translated before the Millennium but go through part of the 7-Year Tribulation and be raptured in the middle of the period.

They assume that the last trump of I Corinthians 15:52 is the seventh trumpet of Revelation 11:15. Since they believe that the seventh trumpet occurs somewhere in the middle of the 7-year tribulation period, they reason that the rapture will be mid-tribulation. However, the trumpets are not the same. In the rapture (I Corinthians 15:51-58: I Thessalonians 4:13-18), the Lord Himself shall descend from heaven with a shout with the voice of the archangel, Michael. During the Great Tribulation, a seventh angel sounds, not Michael the archangel.

However, there is a rapture during the tribulation of the two witnesses of Revelation 11:11, 12)

- ʼAt the **last trump** of the First Resurrection (translation; rapture), the **saints meet Jesus in the air** (I Thessalonians 4:17; I Corinthians 15:52).

- At The First Resurrection, Christ comes **FOR** His saints (I Corinthians 15:51-58).

- At the **seventh trump** of the Great Tribulation, **Jesus prepares for His kingdom reign on earth** (Revelation 11:15).

At Christ's Second Coming, Christ comes **WITH** His saints (Jude 14).

The Last Trump

Again, this Pre-Millennial Mid-Tribulation Rapture group believes that the Church will be translated before the millennium but go through part of the 7-Year Tribulation Period and be raptured in the middle of the period.

Again, the Mid-Tribulationists assume that the last trump of I Corinthians 15:52 is the Seventh Trumpet of Revelation 11:15. Since they believe that the seventh trumpet occurs somewhere in the middle of the 7-year Tribulation Period, they reason that the Rapture will occur "mid-tribulation." The trumpets are not the same. In the Rapture (I Corinthians 15:51-58; I Thessalonians 4:13-18; Titus 2:13), the Lord Himself shall descend from heaven with a shout with the "voice" of Michael the archangel, but during the Great Tribulation, a seventh angel of seven angels sounds with a trumpet, not with a noise as a thundering VOICE of Michael the archangel.

The Seventh Trumpet of Revelation 11:15 is in reference to an ANNOUNCEMENT. Christ is about to set up his millennial kingdom upon earth following the horrendous judgments upon the world. Even the other prior six trumpets also are in the form of ANNOUNCEMNTS pertaining to the anticipation of coming judgments. The Seventh Trumpet has nothing to do with the "change" of earthy bodies to resurrection bodies as in I Corinthians 15:51-58 and I Thessalonians 4:13-18. Again, all six of the trumpet sounds of the seven angels are ANNOUNCEMENTS of imminent "judgments" that are totally unlike the Last Trump of I Corinthians 15:52 which pertains to "rescue" (not judgments during the Tribulation Period) and the CHANGE of the saints of the Church Age (The First Resurrection).

Recapping, the Last Trump of I Corinthians 15:52 is in reference to CHANGE (not an "announcement"). The subject in this chapter is death being conquered by God's resurrection power. Actually, I Corinthians chapter 15 is frequently referred to as the "Resurrection Chapter" of the Bible.

A "Last Trump of God," of course, implies that there must be "a First Trump of God." The Two Silver Trumpets that God instructed Moses to make are models for the Two Trumps of God (Numbers 10:2). Initially, the silver trumpets were used as commands to Israel (assemble for instructions; prepare for war; prepare to move camp; move out camp). The ram's horn (shofar) was used for a trumpet; the sounds (number of short blasts, long blasts, etc) determined the trumpet's instruction.

The First Trump of God at Sinai was called "voice of the trumpet,' **not** the "sound" of the trumpet (Exodus 19:16, 19). This was God's voice booming "as" a great trumpet. The Last Trump is described as "**...**shout, with the **voice** of the archangel, and with the **trump of God** (I Thessalonians 4:16). This trump refers to **a voice as a great trumpet**, not merely a blast from a ram or silver horn. "Voice" is observed in both the First and Last trumps of God (not of seven trumps of seven angels).

We also see the voice "as" a trumpet talking to John after the Church Age has ended and before the 7-Year Tribulation Period begins:

Revelation 4:1: After this (the Church Age) *I looked, and, behold, a door was opened in heaven: and the first **voice** which I heard was **as it were of a trumpet talking** with me; which said, Come up hither, and I will shew thee things which must be hereafter.*

In this text, John was projected into the future about 2,000 years later to the First Resurrection (Rapture) and is shown scenes in Heaven. Then the Seven Seal judgments upon the earth are revealed to John. The true Church (*Lamb's wife; the Bride of Christ*) is nowhere mentioned at all during the judgments of the Tribulation Period; it is only mentioned after all of the judgments upon the world are finished (Revelation 19:7; 21:9).

There is only one version of religion in the world during Daniel's 70th Week of Prophecy (The 7-Year Tribulation Period) and it is pictured in Revelation chapters 18 and 19 as "the great whore that sitteth upon many waters (Revelation 17:1). It is called "MYSTERY BABYON THE GREAT, THE MOTHER OF HARLOTS AND ABOMINATONS OF THE EARTH (Revelation 17:5). The writer calls it The Bride of Antichrist.

Again, the Bride of the Lamb (The Church) will not be upon earth during the 7-Year Tribulation Period which is "The time of Jacob's trouble" (Jeremiah 30:7) and Daniel's 70th Week of Prophecy (Daniel 9:24-27).

- ♦ At the **Last Trump** of the First Resurrection (translation; rapture), the **saints meet Jesus in the air** (I Thessalonians 4:17; I Corinthians 15:52). This is when Christ comes **FOR** His saints (I Corinthians 15:51-58) and **takes them to Heaven.** For them, there is **no more death;** however if this was a picture during any part of the 7-Year Tribulation Period, there would be death for believers refusing the mark of the beast.

- ♦ At the **Seventh Trump** of the seventh angel of the Great Tribulation, **Jesus prepares for His Kingdom reign on earth** (Revelation 11:15). Shortly after the sound of the

Seventh Trump, Christ comes **WITH** His saints. This is at the Second Coming of Christ (Jude 14).

Too, if either Mid-Tribulation or Post-Tribulation Raptures were true, the Church would be expecting to look for the treaty signing between Antichrist and Israel. The Church would be expecting to see the Abomination of Desolation; the Church would expect to see a combination of events which occur during the last week of Daniel's 70 Weeks which is Jewish time and unrelated to the Church. However, the Church is admonished to look for Christ, not Antichrist and the Tribulation Period (Titus 2:13; Philippians 3:20).

Pre-Millennial Post-Tribulation Rapture

3.) **Pre-Millennial Post-Tribulation Rapture:** This group believes that the Church will be translated before the millennium and after the 7-year Tribulation Period.

Probably, the main reason for this belief is based upon Revelation 20:4-6 where it is said that there is a thousand years between "they that lived and reigned with Christ" and "the rest of the dead that lived not again until the thousand years were finished." But these that lived and reigned with Christ had been beheaded **during** the Great Tribulation because of their witness of Jesus and His Word. They had refused to worship the beast or receive his mark upon their forehead or in their hands. Christ's witnesses were beheaded at least three and one-half years or more after the translation (rapture) of the main body of resurrection saints. Although these tribulation saints **had part** (Revelation 20:6) in the first resurrection (as gleanings of the resurrection harvest), they were not translated with the "harvest" resurrection **before** the Great Tribulation began. That would have been before they had even been slain, which occurred during the last half of the 7-year tribulation. Yes, there will be a post tribulation rapture/resurrection for those who were slain during the tribulation period, but the Church has already been resurrected.

Post-Millennial Rapture

4.) Post-Millennial Rapture: This group believes that Christ will return at the end of the Millennium and translate the Church. However, Christ does not return because He is already present and rules on the throne of David in Jerusalem during the entire millennium.

Advocates of Post-millennialism believe that the Church will prosper and extend until the world is converted. They misinterpret Matthew 13:33 by likening the Gospel as leaven which expands "till the whole world was leavened." The Gospel is not likened to leaven because leaven is a type of expanding **hypocrisy, evil, and false doctrine** (Exodus 12:15; Matthew 16:6, 12; Mark 8:15; Galatians 5:9; Luke 12:1; I Corinthians 5:7-8).

The Gospel is "the power of God unto salvation" (Romans 1:16).

Pre-Millennial Partial-Rapture Theory

5.) Pre-Millennial Partial-Rapture Theory: This group believes that only a select group of spiritual Christians will be translated before the beginning of the 7-year Tribulation Period. However, if any **member** of the body of Christ were missing, the body would be blemished, wrinkled, or spotted. Contrariwise, Christ's body will be without spot or wrinkle (Ephesians 1:22-23; 2:16; 4:4, 16; 5:27-32; I Corinthians 12:12-27).

A body without all of its members is equivalent to a mutated body. An imperfect body (bride) is unacceptable to God. God would only accept the OT sacrifices that were without spot or blemish.

We are told in I Corinthians 15:51 that "we **all** shall be changed," not a select group of believers. All means "all" inclusive, not "exclusive" of some

An "alleged" select group of believers is similar to the belief of those advocates that teach that a special group of "overcomers" only will be in the First Resurrection (translation; rapture). Of course, all saved people are overcomers in the sense of the new birth which is salvation.

> *I John 4:4: Ye are of God, little children, and have **overcome** them: because greater is he that is in you, than he that is in the world.*

> *I John 5:4: For whatsoever is born of God **overcometh** the world: and this is the victory that overcometh the world, even our faith.*

> *I John 5:5: Who is he that **overcometh** the world, but he that believeth that Jesus is the Son of God?*

No one that has trusted Christ as their Saviour is going to be eliminated from the First Resurrection (rapture) because they are less spiritual than another believer.

No-Rapture Theory

6.) No-Rapture Theory: This group is anti-rapture; they do not believe in a translation or rapture of any kind. This is tantamount (equal) to a plain denial of The First Resurrection.

The deniers of the rapture have great difficulty in explaining the translation of Enoch and Elijah in the Old Testament and also the Church in the New Testament (I Corinthians 15:51-58; I Thessalonians 4:13-18). Again, the Rapture and First Resurrection are one and the same.

The writer agrees with the *pre-millennial pre-tribulation* position (Belief No. 1 above).

(**NOTE # 1:** The English word "rapture" is taken from the Latin Bible's "rapto" and means "to catch away" or "catch away in clouds.")

Harlot Church

(**NOTE # 2:** The **"harlot church"** will continue for a while during the Tribulation Period – Revelation 13:12-15; Revelation 17-18. The writer prefers to call this abomination **"The Bride of Antichrist."**

She is a harlot, not a virgin. This **MOTHER OF HARLOTS and** matriarch of false religions, attempts to impersonate the true church. The virgin-bride of Christ \is without spot, wrinkle or blemish – Ephesians 5:27.)

All orthodox (conforming to established Christian doctrines) saints of Christendom believe in some version of the Rapture (First Resurrection). The big difference is in **how** and **when** they perceive the translation to occur (as noted above). The only religionists that deny a rapture (First Resurrection) in Christendom are modernists, heretics, and teachers of cultic religions.

One false prophet and mocker of the rapture is **Arnold Murray** of Gravette, Arkansas. The writer would hope that this false prophet (who has espoused many other false dogmas) has not gone too far beyond God's mercy.

Light on the Order of Prophetical Events

Does the OT Shed light on the Order of Prophetical Events?

Yes! Actually, all prophecy is associated in some way to Israel and may give the chronological order of events.

The *Seven Feasts of Leviticus 23* is one example of prophetic chronology. The OT order was:

1) Passover

2.) Feast of Unleavened Bread

3) Firstfruits

4.) Pentecost {Feast of Weeks}

5) Trumpets

6.) Day of Atonement

7) Feast of Tabernacles {Sukkot}

Applying this *OT chronological order* to the NT, we may have the possible application:

➢ Feast # 1, **Passover**, represents Messiah's sacrificial death. Christ is our Passover. (I Corinthians 5:7)

➢ Feast # 2, **Feast of Unleavened Bread**, represent Messiah's sinless blood offering and communion.

➢ Feast # 3, **Feast of First-fruits**, represents Christ's Resurrection (and perhaps of the OT saints (Matthew 27:51-53).

➢ Feast # 4, **Pentecost Trumpets** {Feast of Weeks}, which was one day after seven weeks (50) of OT Passover. Pentecost represents the descent of the Holy Spirit and His continual indwelling of the NT believer.

➢ Feast # 5, **Trumpets**, represents the First Resurrection (Rapture) of which Christ was the First of the Firstfruits

➢ Feast # 6, **Day of Atonement**, represents The Great Tribulation which is less a feast and more a fast. The collective sin of Israel for a whole year was brought to remembrance that it may be atoned for...that as NT partakers of His forgiveness might rejoice and carry out His commandments.

➢ Feast # 7, **Feast of Tabernacles** {Sukkot} represents the Millennium when Jesus dwells with His flock.

If a person says that the First Resurrection (Rapture) comes after the Tribulation Period (Post-Rapture theory), they are saying that the sixth feast comes before the fifth feast. In *Leviticus 23*, the Lord called the feasts, "My appointed times, "My appointed feast, "My set feast." Thus the fifth feast (Trumpets) must come before the sixth feast (Day of Atonement).

Because the Feasts of Leviticus 23 symbolize NT events, the order of the OT feasts can aid us in determining the order (chronology) of NT events.

CHAPTER 15

THE "ONLY HOPE" OF MANKIND

The last great hope of every person living today is to be in the First Resurrection - (Revelation 20:6). It cannot be over emphasized that **a person must be born again to be included in The First Resurrection,**

> *John 3:1-8: There was a man of the Pharisees, named Nocodemus, a ruler of the Jews: The same came to Jesus by night, and said unto him Rabbi, we know that thou art a teacher come from God: for no man can do these miracles that thou doest, except God be with him. Jesus answered and said unto him, Verily, verily, I say unto thee,* **Except a man be born again, he cannot see the kingdom of God.** *Nicodemus saith unto him, How can a man be born when he is old? Can he enter the second time into his mother's womb, and be born. Jesus answered, Verily, verily, I say unto thee,* **Except a man be born of water and of the Spirit, he cannot enter into the kingdom of God.** *That which is born of the flesh is flesh; and that which is born of the Spirit is spirit. Marvel not that I said unto thee,* **Ye must be born again.** *The wind bloweth where it listeth (chooses or pleases), and thou hearest the sound thereof, but canst not tell whence it cometh, and whither it goeth: so is every one that is born of the Spirit.*

Except a Man be Born of Water

(Water: Water symbolizes the Word of God - Psalms 119:9; Ezekiel 36:25-27; John 3:5; 7:37-39; 15:3; Ephesians 5:25, 26; Titus 3:5-7; James 1:18; I Peter 1:22, 23; Romans 10:17; Ephesians 2:8. The conjunction "and" [Greek "kai"] can also be translated as "even" meaning the same.)

We were born first by water (amniotic fluid of natural birth); but we are born again by the water of the Word of God. It is by hearing, believing, and obeying the Word of God -(Romans 10:11, 14, 17)

> *I Peter 1:23:* ***Being born again****, not of corruptible seed, but of incorruptible,* ***by the Word of God****, which liveth and abideth for ever.*

Again, our natural birth (generation) is by water (amniotic fluid) but the new birth (regeneration) is by the Holy Spirit.

See the writer's booklet, "Does Water Baptism Save?"

> *I Corinthians 12:13: For by one* ***Spirit*** *are we all baptized into one body, whether we be Jews or Gentiles, whether we be bond or free; and have been all made to drink into one* ***Spirit****.*

Of course, the **Spirit of God** and the **Word of God** work co-jointly together through faith. So then faith cometh by hearing, and hearing by the Word of God (Romans 10:17).

> *Ephesians 2:8-9: For by grace are ye saved through* ***faith****; and that not of yourselves: it is the gift of God: Not of works, lest any man should boast.*

> *I Corinthians 1:17-18: For Christ sent me* ***not to baptize*** *but to preach the gospel: not with wisdom of words, lest the cross of Christ should be made of none effect. For the preaching of the cross is to them that perish foolishness; but unto us which are saved it is the power of God.*

(**NOTE**: If baptism saved or helped to save anyone, I Corinthians 1:17 would have no meaning or application whatsoever.)

> *Ephesians 2:15:* ***Having abolished*** *in his flesh the enmity, even the law of commandments contained in* ***ordinances****; for to make in himself of twain one new man, so making peace.*

> *Colossians 2:14:* ***Blotting out*** *the handwriting of* ***ordinances*** *that was against us which was*

contrary to us, and took it out of the way, nailing it to his cross.

These verses from *Ephesians* and *Colossians* are alluding to Israel's having been under the law of *ceremonial* ordinances which the Jews were required to honor; however, the outward observance of ordinances did not save them. These ordinances of the Mosaic Law were of the flesh and not of faith. The law can only condemn by pointing out our sins (Galatians 2:21; 3:10-14, 19-27; I Corinthians 12:13). Ceremonies were only part of the Mosaic Law. Actually, the Law worked death and thundered the judgment of God to all that could not keep "all" of the law.

Neither are the New Testament ordinances (Communion and Baptism) sacraments given to save souls. The NT ordinances are pictures or symbols of redemption given to believers (who are already saved) to observe in obedience to His command.

Where Does It All End?

Man's ultimate earthly end is his body in the "grave" and his soul either in Hell or **Heaven. Actually, death (and judgment) is prophesied many times in Scriptures:**

*Hebrews 9:27: And as it is appointed unto men once to **die**; but after that the **judgment**.*

Death is the separation of the soul and spirit of man from his body. At death, the soul and spirit of man departs from earth and returns to God from whence it came

As pertaining to death, the editor of the *Seventh Trumpet* magazine often told the true story of a traveler who, wandering through an old country cemetery, came upon a grave that caught his attention. It was marked with a stone, and upon it were these lines of poetry:

Pause, stranger, as you pass me by;

As you are now, so once was I;

As I am now, you too shall be,

So prepare for death and follow me.

The stranger paused a moment. As he thought of eternity, the suffering of the lost, then of the home of the redeemed with Christ in Heaven, he could not leave the cemetery till he wrote the two last lines:

To follow you, I am not content,

Until I know which place you went.

Actually, the grave is not the end of man. The grave is man's final testimonial to earth. Death is the doorway of **everlasting life** or **everlasting damnation**. God's perfect sacrifice for sinful man has been offered on Calvary's cross. A sinner has only to reach out by faith and receive God's gift of eternal life (Ephesians 2:8-9; Romans 6:23; 10:13).

Wake-Up Calls

◆ Gay Day Celebrations Parades at Disney, New Orleans Mardi Gras (and South Carolina University)

Jerusalem celebrates World Pride from August 6 through 12, 2006. Judge Tzur ruled that the holy city of Zion had been discriminating in its cultural funding practices, so ordered the city to pay 350,000 shekels (approximately $80,000.00 in American currency) to the Jerusalem Open House for Pride and Tolerance because it had ignored the sodomites in the past (years 2003-2005). Hotels seeking to cash in on the affair are the Gloria, Inbal, Jerusalem Inn, Jerusalem Tower, Prima Royale, Sheraton Plaza, and Argon Hostel. All six are offering the Sodomites special rates!

It is not uncommon to see large groups of sodomite protesters in public demonstrations.

Many apostate religions are even endorsing the abominable practice of sodomy for their "so-called" ministers (harlots and drunkards have far better sense).

◆ Insurance for sodomite partners

◆ Polygamists (Mormons and/or Latter Day Saints) are endeavoring to be recognized as Christian, and according to one source, about 47% of "professing" Christians believe they are Christian (Note the word "professing").

◆ White House catering to sodomites

◆ DC Comics planned to come out with a new Bat Woman comic in which she will be a lesbian

◆ White House catering to abortion

◆ Missile disaster in Russia (missiles stolen and unaccounted for)

◆ Hillary re-defined family as village

◆ People and government confused about gender of marriage partners

◆ Robin Hood socialistic governmental mentality (nanny state) not provided for in the Constitution nor in the Word of God (2 Thessalonians 3:10).

◆ Pontius Pilate lives today (What is truth?...John 18:38)

◆ Euthanasia will one day be law. Abortion is the parent killing the child. Euthanasia is the child killing the parent.

◆ Over one-million abortions annually (over 54 million slaughtered since 1973 Roe vs. Wade and replaced by over 20 million illegal unpatriotic aliens.

◆ Clinton/s Armed Forces sodomite push

◆ Protestant religions (Anglican/Episcopalian; Lutheran, Presbyterian; Methodist; etc.) endorsing sodomite ministers. Many are already in the priesthood of Catholic churches.

◆ The Episcopal Peace Fellowship recently awarded its highest honor to Canon Naim Atteek, a Palestinian who has denied the right of Israel to even exist.

◆ Nations are now endorsing sodomy relationships and marriage (Spain, Switzerland, Canada, Netherlands, Norway, and some states of America headed that way...)

◆ Diseases are no longer caused by germs. Everything now is termed a disease. Even "road rage" is now classified as a disease (the asylum is now run by the inmates). When the writer was in grade school, we were taught that diseases were caused by germs. If drunkards are the result of diseases sold in bottles (called "booze"), maybe we should sue the government for spreading and profiting from diseases.

◆ Iran is vigorously striving to make nuclear weapons and the Muslim nations are committed to the destruction of Israel.

◆ Gershon Salomon is heading a group dedicated to the laying of the Jewish Temple foundation. This location is presumably occupied by the Islamic holy shrine, the Dome of the Rock. The destruction of the Muslim shrine would set off a certain "all out war" of the Muslim world. Perhaps God will use an earthquake to destroy it.

The Only Escape is the Lord's Salvation

*Hebrews 2:3-4: How shall we escape, **if we neglect so great salvation**; which at the first began to be spoken by the Lord, and was confirmed unto us by them that heard him; God also bearing them witness, both with signs and wonders, and with divers miracles, and gifts of the Holy Ghost, according to his own will?*

Luke 13:3: I tell you, Nay: but, except ye repent, ye shall all likewise perish.

Ephesians 2:8-9: For by grace are ye saved through faith; and that not of yourselves: it is the gift of God: Not of works, lest any man should boast.

Romans 10:9-10, 13: That if thou shalt confess with thy mouth the Lord Jesus, and shalt believe in thine heart that God hath raised him from the dead, thou shalt be saved. For with the heart man believeth unto righteousness; and with the mouth confession is made unto salvation. For whosoever shall call upon the name of the Lord shall be saved.

Matthew 11:28-30: Come unto me, all ye that labour and are heavy laden, and I will give you rest. Take my yoke upon you, and learn of me; for I am meek and lowly in heart: and ye shall find rest unto your souls. For my yoke is easy, and my burden is light.

John 3:36: He that believeth on the Son hath everlasting life: and he that believeth not the Son shall not see life; but the wrath of God abideth on him.

For the testimony of Jesus is the Spirit of Prophecy - Revelation 19:10.

<u>The Spirit of Prophecy and the Spirit of Christ are One and the same:</u>

I Peter 1:11: Searching what, or what manner of time the Spirit of Christ which was in them did signify, when it testified beforehand the sufferings of Christ and the glory that should follow. -See 2 Peter 1:21

Clarence Larkin says of the Bible, "Man could not have written if he would, and would not have written it if he could." (*Prophecy illuminates the future by forecasting it* - Clarence Larkin)

The World Condition Today and the Future World to Come

The nations are ripe for the acceptance of the **Antichrist** and his henchman **the false prophet** of Revelation 13:1-18; 16:13; 19:20; 20:10. World conditions are now to the point that Antichrist could easily come on the scene with everything already set up and in place for him to dictate world policy. Technology in many fields has expanded exponentially. The writer believed and predicted (based upon the Word of God) in the 1980's that advances in electronics and chemistry was only in the infant stages. Of course, the Bible predicted that this great increase of knowledge would occur (Daniel 12:4).

When this writer was a boy, his neighborhood was quite primitive (compared to today). Many neighborhood streets outside the city were unpaved (dirt) and consequently many times were watered down in the evening to help prevent dust from penetrating into the neighborhood houses. Most people in the neighborhood walked nearly everywhere they went because most people did not have cars. Actually, there were several families in the writer's neighborhood that used horses and wagons. In the summertime when young boys were walking a paved main highway, it was not unusual (and it was a welcome thing) for them to sometimes catch a ride on the back of a horse-pulled wagon (the pavement was very hot on bare feet). The point that the writer is trying to make is that in the writer's short lifetime, technology has advanced from horses and wagons to complex rockets placing a man on the moon. This is much knowledge increased in just one generation, more than all other generations combined since the beginning of the world. In all of history, there has never been as much advancement in science and technology as in the writer's generation. Man can fly faster than sound travels and very little is thought of it. Man can send and receive both sound and pictures through the airways at very distant locations and little is thought about it; small hand-held cell phones can perform about any function you desire as: wireless telephone; calculator; computer; still-picture camera; movie camera; TV viewing; internet; mapping; etc. (and the only thing that grabs mans' attention is when the monthly bills arrive). One expert said that the modern hand-held cellphones have greater technology than existed in computers used in the moon landing.

There are reports that most of the people in civilized countries (5-6 six billion) are registered on super master-computers in Europe. Even tiny microchips imbedded in or placed on an object allows anybody or anything upon earth to be located within a few feet. And with all this advancement, the evil, rebellious character of man has not changed one iota. Men are still proud, rebellious, vile, jealous, murderous, and atheistic.

Nearly the whole world is unfairly prejudiced against Israel. Many Muslim nations deny Israel the right to exist as a nation of people. Even our new president is leaning away from supporting Israel's basic rights and lending support to radical Muslims. Most of our elected politicians are not worth a dime-a-dozen and are only interesting in "political correctness" and "reelection." A conglomerate of nations (such as G-20, a group of 20 nations) are now meeting with the aim of solving the world's economic problems.

The TV has just about turned into a foul sewer line piping in raw filth and we become slowly conditioned in allowing the garbage to be piped into our homes. Much of the mass national news reports are mostly "news commentaries, news propaganda, half-facts, and omissions of facts." The opinionated news reports are constantly tainted by politically correct, biased, leftwing liberals and Marxists. Most of the news reports are geared to control our minds to dwell upon whatever subject they wish us to talk about. Many times, the news propaganda is a "red herring" (planted false clue) to divert our attention away from more important issues that need to be addressed. The mass media is a number one culprit in promoting the left-wing agenda.

There are many disloyal to our Constitution. To name some of them: liberals; college professors; communists; pinkos; the national news media, illegal immigrants; Muslims; phony religionists; liberal "so called" preachers; the Hollywood cess-pool; disgruntled Mexicans; Islamic infiltrators; adversaries of the First and Second Amendments to the Constitution; left wingers; atheists; environmentalists (euphemism: tree huggers and mother-earth kissers); abortionists (baby butchers). Now the writer is aware that this not 100 % true for all of these people involved and too, many are naively deceived pawns of The New World Order.

These things are just some of the precursors announcing the soon arrival of the man of sin.

CHAPTER 16

RUSSIA AND HER ALLIES WILL SEEK TO INVADE ISRAEL

Before the attack upon Israel by Russian led hordes, there appears to be another large- scale battle as described in Psalms 83:4, 6-8, 12. These nations mentioned in Psalms 83 do not appear to be the same nations as those in Ezekiel 38. Most of these nations of Psalms 83 appear to be Muslims. This war may occur right before the beginning of Daniel's 70th week of Prophecy (The 7-Year Tribulation Period; The Time of Jacob's Trouble - Jeremiah 30:7).

Probably sometime immediately before or right after The First Resurrection (Translation; Rapture), Russia (Rosh) and her hordes of Jew haters will attempt to invade Israel. At a time on earth when the entire world has been greatly polarized against Israel, radical Muslims led by Islamist controlled Russia and her racist allies, will think the time is ripe to "take a spoil, and to take a prey." At this time, America is most likely greatly weakened by economic failure, internal moral decay, political corruption, and traitors.

Of course, a harlot world religion will have been established at this time (Revelation chapters 17 and 18).

Ezekiel 38:

1. *AND the word of the LORD (Jehovah) came unto me* (Ezekiel), *saying,*

2. *Son of man, set thy face against Gog* (prince), *the land of Magog* (land of Gog), *the chief prince* (prince of Rosh or Russia) *of Meshech* (Moscow) *and Tubal* (Tobolsk), *and prophesy against him,*

3. *And say, Thus saith the Lord God; Behold, I am against thee, O Gog, the chief prince of Meshech and Tubal:*

4. And I will turn thee back, And put hooks into thy jaws, and I will bring thee forth, and all thine army, **horses** and horsemen, all of them clothed with all sorts *of armour, even* a great company with bucklers and shields, all of them handling swords:

(Some think Ezekiel spoke of "tanks and guns" as "horses and swords," in terms of things he knew, but also summarized it as "all sorts of armour." Others believe that an EMP [Electromagnetic Pulse] bomb will be exploded overhead that destroys all electrical functions of communications, machinery and automotive equipment. They say this explains the necessity of the usage of horses and horsemen.)

5. Persia *(Iran)*, Ethiopia *(parts of Africa)* and Libya with them; all of them with shield and helmet:

6. Gomer *(Germany)*, and all his bands; the house of Togarmah *(Turkey/Armenia)* of the north quarters, and all his bands: and many people (mostly Muslims) with thee.

7. Be thou prepared, and prepare for thyself, thou, and all thy company that are assembled unto thee, and be thou a guard unto them.

8.   After many days (over 2,000 years) thou shalt be visited: in the latter years thou shalt come into the land (Israel) *that is* brought back from the sword, *and is* gathered out of many people *(many nations where they were dispersed)*, against the mountains of Israel, which have been always waste; but it is brought forth out of the nations, and they shall <u>dwell safely</u> all of them *(perhaps after the 7-year covenant with the Antichrist)*.

9.   Thou shalt ascend and come like a storm, thou shalt be like a cloud *(perhaps as a swarm or possibly an aerial attack)* to cover the land, thou, and all thy bands, and many people with thee.

10.   And thou shalt say, I will go up to the land of unwalled villages; I will go to them that are at rest, that <u>dwell</u>

<u>safely</u>, all of them dwelling <u>without walls</u>, and having neither bars nor gates,

(Apparently, Israel can only assume to dwell safely after a 7-year covenant with the Antichrist. Obviously, there is now no present peace and they are constantly bombarded with rockets and other terrorist attacks.)

11.   To take s spoil, and to take a prey; to turn thine hand upon the desolate places *that are now* inhabited, and upon the people *that are* gathered out of the nations, which have gotten cattle and goods, that dwell in the midst of the land.

(Some think to seize the minerals of the dead sea which are valued at over a trillion dollars. Others think that large reserves of oil will be discovered in Israel.)

12.   Sheba *(Yemen/Arabia)*, and Dedan *(Edom; Idemea; shores of the Persian Gulf)*, and the merchants of Tarshish *(Spain; Phoenicia)*, with all the young lions thereof, shall say unto thee, Art thou come to take a spoil? hast thou gathered thy company to take a prey? To carry away silver and gold, to take away cattle and goods, to take a great spoil?

13.   And it shall come to pass at the Same time when Gog shall come against the land of Israel, saith the Lord God, *that* my fury shall come up in m face.

14.   For in my jealousy and in the fire of my wrath have I spoken, Surely in that day there shall be a great shaking in the land of Israel.

Ezekiel 39:

1. THEREFORE, thou son of man, prophesy against Gog, and say, Thus saith the Lord God; Behold, I *am* against thee, O Gog, the chief prince of Meshech and Tubal:

There is also a final revolt of the "Gog" nations at the close of the kingdom age Revelation 20:7-9.

2. And I will turn thee back, and leave but the sixth part of thee, and will cause thee to come up from the north parts, and will bring thee upon the mountains of Israel:

Russia and her Muslim counterparts will fail in their attempt to invade Israel.

3   Thou shall fall upon the mountains of Israel, thou, and all thy bands, and the people that is with thee: I will give thee unto the ravenous birds of every sort, and *to* the beasts of the field to be devoured.

This prophecy belongs to the future "day of Jehovah" (Isaiah 2:10-22; Revelation 19:11-21) and leads up to World War III, the battle of Armageddon (Revelation 16:14-16; 19:19). See also Zechariah 12:1-4; 14:1-9; Matthew 24:14-30; Revelation 14:14-20; 19:17-21.

Muslim Hatred

The writer is well aware of the intense Muslim hatred against Israel and is not surprised at their part in the attempt to invade Israel in the last days. For some time, the writer also wondered why other nations of Europe would be joined with Russia in this Gog and Magog assault upon Israel. The answer probably lies in the fact that these non-Muslim nations of Europe will be largely influenced by the oil-producing Islamic countries. These European countries will also be increase in large Muslim population numbers. Without oil, most nations could not compete on the world market that demands machinery and moving vehicles.

Some say that the Muslim religion is the fastest growing religion in the world today. In several countries of Europe, Muslims have already exerted great influence (as Muslim sharia law) on governments and international affairs.

According to one report, in order for a country to maintain its culture, the fertility rate (birth rate) for each family must be 2.11 for each. The report said that a country with a family fertility rate of 1.9 is never repaired and a country with a family fertility rate of 1.3 is impossible to repair. The report says: France has a family fertility rate of 1.8; England 1.6; Greece 1.3; Germany 1.3; Italy 1.2; Spain 1.1. The report says that 31 countries of Europe have an average 1.35 fertility rate. However, immigration of Muslims and their rapid fertility rate is filling the void of civilized nations of the earth. Canada and America was rated at a 1.6 fertility rate. However, the fertility rate of Muslims was much higher than a 2.1 rate which is necessary to sustain a country's culture (patriotism; morality; religion; et al). The fertility rate of Islam was listed as a whopping 8.1. So, what is the consequence? In a couple of generations, the exponential birth explosion of Muslims will give them the political power needed to influence or even rule governments. One Muslim leader stated that Islam did not need to rely upon terrorism and weapons of war to overcome the non-Muslim nations but they will rule by population increase. So the bottom line is that the Islamic population increase in Russia and European nations will fuel the flames to invade Israel in the last days. It does not matter if these numeric fertility rates are somewhat inaccurate because the expansion of Islam is a national fact. Ishmael's descendants have always been the enemy of Israel and will continue to be until Jesus puts down those nations which are controlled by Islam's fanatical hatred.

Slowly, but surely, non-Muslim nations are allowing Muslims to practice their Islamic sharia law (*the body of Islamic religious law*). Sharia deals with day-to-day Muslim matters: politics; economics; banking; business; contracts; family; sexuality; hygiene; social issues (*sharia means "The path to a watering hole"*). Sharia is a religious code of living in the same way the Bible offers a moral system for Christians. Sharia law is both a unmerciful bloody religion and a political philosophy that contrasts with Christian tenets.

➤ Husbands may hit their wives (Quran 4:34)

➤ A woman's testimony counts ½ that of man

➢ An injured plaintiff may exact legal revenge, a physical eye for a physical eye (Quran 5:45)

➢ A male and female thief must have a hand cut off (Quran 5:38)

➢ Highway robbers should be crucified or mutilated (Quran 5:33)

➢ Homosexuals must be executed

➢ Unmarried fornicators are to be whipped and adulterers be stoned to death (Quran 24:2)

➢ Death for Muslim and possible death for non-Muslim critics of Muhammad and the Quran and even sharia itself.

➢ Apostates to be killed for criticizing clerical rule (*after given time to repent*) – Quran Sura 9:11-12.

➢ Islam commands offensive and aggressive and unjust jihad ranging from small assassination hit squads to kill anyone who insults Muhammad (*sharia law is presently being pushed in Canada and Australia*)

➢ Women and children are enslaved and can either be sold or Muslim men may marry the women, since their marriages are automatically annulled upon their capture. Jihadists may have sex with slave women.

➢ People of the Book (Jews and Christians) had three options (Sura 9:29):

Fight and die; convert and pay a forced 'charity' or zakat tax; keep biblical faith and pay a jizya or poll tax.

Political Islam advocates jihad to achieve world domination.

It appears that soon there will be war between Israel and Iran (Persia). Israel knows that their very existence depends upon defeating Iran's nuclear capability which is rapidly materializing. After America's near total economic collapse, Israel will have little or no support and will be forced to fight to exist.

Signs Point Toward 'Cataclysmic" War in Middle East (Cyberspace 5-11-09)

A former top American intelligence official agrees with a Messianic pastor that major and possibly calamitous events will unfold in the Middle East in the coming year

"I think within 12 months something is going to happen, one way or another," said retired Lt. Gen. William Boykin, who served as deputy undersecretary of defense for intelligence from 2003 to 2007.

His concerns are echoed by best-selling novelist Joel C. Rosenberg. Whose works have uncannily foreshadowed real events including 9/11.

"I don't know how much time we have. I believe a cataclysmic war is coming in the Middle East," he said.

Messianic pastor Mark Biltz of El Shaddai ministries in Puyallup, Wash. garnered attention last year with his announcement of the discovery of a rare sequence of lunar and

Solar eclipses, a "tetrad," are all falling on key feast days on the Jewish calendar over a two-year period.

The last time that happened, the Jews recaptured Jerusalem, Biltz said. "The time before that [was] 1949, 1950, right after they became a nation. But both times it was tied around a major war."

Additional signs this year and next portend more of the same, according to Biltz.

"The sun and the moon were God's signals to us," he said. "When they fall on his divine appointments, He's trying to tell us that we need to look to him and hear what he's saying."

While Biltz and other messianic believers watch the heavens, "others are watching the headlines and getting the same message," station KMPH in Fresno, Calif., reported.

Gen. Boykin told a station reporter at a conference in San Diego that he foresees "something" happening in the coming year and added: "I'm watching the Iranian nuclear program very carefully. No one really knows how long, I don't even think the Iranian themselves know how long it will take them to have a deliverable nuclear weapon, but they're moving there rapidly."

Author Rosenberg, who was an adviser to then-Israeli Prime Minister Benjamin Netanyahu in the 1990s, foresees a cataclysm in the near future, and he has been remarkably prescient (to know beforehand) in his books.

For instance, his New York Times best-seller "The Last Jihad" describes the hijacking of a jet by radical Islamic terrorists who use it to launch a kamikaze attack on an American city. That leads to a war with Iraq's Saddam Hussein over terrorism and weapons of mass destruction.

"I wrote those chapters nine months before September 11, 2001," Rosenberg told KMPH at the conference.

His book "The Last Days" begins with a U.S. diplomatic convoy driving into Gaza on a peacekeeping mission. The convoy is attacked by terrorists. Six days before the book went on sale in October 2003, an American diplomatic convoy driving into Gaza was attacked by terrorists.

The book also foreshadowed a civil war among Palestinians similar to the hostilities that later erupted between Hamas and Fatah.

Whether or not these things occur at designated times or not is not that important. The issue is that the seriousness of the potential for them to occur. Even political experts are exhibiting fear of that probability.

The writer thinks that it is a glaring fact that over 60 million babies (1973-2012) butchered in America (with the blessing of our own government) has been largely replaced with illegals and Muslims. The illegals will soon qualify for social security benefits even though they may have never contributed a penny into the social security fund. The Muslim religion is rapidly gaining prominence and power in America (thanks to our Muslim president). If the 54 million aborted children had lived, they would have had some degree of patriotism, but their replacement by illegals and Muslims is demolishing our Constitution, destroying our economy, and corrupting our Judeo-Christian morals. Patriotism is nearly obsolete in America.

Our own government is forcing its hard working citizens to bail out the bankrupt institutions and the fat cats of higher income for their own stupid mistakes. And on the political scene the ones responsible for causing the national economic crisis are the ones trying to take credit for solving what they themselves created. Of course, there is a conspiracy to "internationalize" America by first bankrupting her. Out of nowhere, it appears that the backwards communist nation of China owns America (*China owns the largest portion of America's debt*). Our governmental "red tape" severely hinders American business but is very careful to protect foreign trade. We have "inmates running the institution" instead of people with common sense with the fear of God. These leftist liberals care not for patriotism and free American principles.

This writer is thankful for Bible prophecy for we know the end in the beginning. Of course, Jesus Himself will smite the gathered Gentile nations and then establish His millennial kingdom in Jerusalem. The Jewish nation will also be spiritually established and receive their true Messiah in which they had officially rejected over two millennia before.

CHAPTER 17

THE GEORGIA GUIDESTONES

The New World Order Foreshadowed

As mentioned previously, on one of the highest hilltops in Elberton County Georgia stands a huge granite monument engraved in eight different languages. On the four giant stones that support the common capstone are 10 guides, or commandments. That monument is alternately referred to as the Georgia Guidestones, or The American Stonehenge. Though relatively unknown to most people, it is an important link to the Occult Hierarchy that dominates the world in which we live.

The origin of that strange monument is shrouded in mystery because no one knows the true identity of the man, or men, who commissioned its construction. All that is known for certain is that in June 1979, a well-dressed, articulate stranger visited the office of the Elberton Granite Finishing Company and announced that he wanted to build an edifice to transmit a message to mankind. He identified himself as R. C. Christian, but it soon became apparent that R. C. Christian was not his real name. He said that he represented a group of men who wanted to offer direction to humanity, but to date, almost two decades later, no one knows who R. C. Christian was or the names of those he represented.

Messages Engraved on the Georgia Guidestones

Several things are apparent. The messages engraved on the Georgia Guidestones deal with four major fields:

(1)   Governance and the establishment of a world government

(2)   Population and reproduction control

(3)   The environment and man's relationship to nature, and

(4)   Spirituality

In the public library in Elberton, a book written by R. C. Christian was found. It says that the monument was erected in recognition of Thomas Paine and the occult philosophy he espoused (Thomas Paine's book "The Age of Reason" was intended to destroy the Judeo-Christian beliefs upon which our country was founded). The Georgia Guidestones are used for occult ceremonies and mystic celebrations to this very day.

<u>The Message of the Georgia Guidestones (engraved in 8 different languages – English, Spanish, Swahili, Hindi, Hebrew, Arabic, Chinese, Russian)</u>:

1. Maintain humanity under 500,000,000 in perpetual balance with nature.

2. Guide reproduction wisely – improving fitness and diversity.

3. Unite humanity with a living new language.

4. Rule passion – faith – tradition – and all things with tempered reason.

5. Protect people and nations with fair laws and just courts.

6. Let all nations rule internally resolving external disputes in a world court.

7. Avoid petty laws and useless officials.

8. Balance personal rights with social duties.

9. Prize truth – beauty – love – seeking harmony with the infinite.

10. Be not a cancer on the earth – Leave room for nature – Leave room for nature.

Limiting the population of the earth to 500 million will require the extermination of over nine-tenths of the world's population.

The American Stonehenge's reference to establishing a world court foreshadows the current move to create an International Criminal Court and The World Government.

The Guidestones' emphasis on preserving nature anticipates the Environmental Movement of the 1990's and today.

The reference to "seeking harmony with the infinite" reflects the current effort to replace Judeo-Christian beliefs with a new spirituality.

The Georgia Guidestones' message foreshadowed the current drive for Sustainable Development. Any time you hear the phrase "Sustainable Development" used, you should substitute the term "Socialism" to be able to understand what is intended.

The similarity between the ideas engraved on the Georgia Guidestones and those espoused in The Earth Charter reflect the common origins of both. The Earth Charter was compiled under the direction of Michal Gorbachev and Maurice Strong.

Yoko Ono the widow of John Lennon, was recently quoted as saying, "I want people to know about the stones…We're headed toward a world where we might blow ourselves up and maybe the globe will not exist…it's a nice time to reaffirm ourselves, knowing all the beautiful things that are in this country and the Georgia Guidestones symbolize that."

The Georgian Guidestones signify a New World Order:

(1)   Dramatically reducing the world population (over nine-tenths).

(2)   Promoting environmentalism (tree huggers; earth kissers; nature worshippers).

(3)   Establishing a world government (with anti-Christ as the political head).

(4)   Promoting a new spirituality (humanism; warmed-over paganism).

Location of The Georgia Guidestones:

The Guidestones are located on a hilltop in Elberton, Georgia, approximately 90 miles east of Atlanta, 45 miles from Athens, Georgia, and 9 miles north of the center of Elberton. The stones are standing on a rise a short distance to the east of Georgia Highway 77 (Hartwell Highway). The turn-off is identified by a street sign as "Guidestones Rd."

Why Interest in a Bible Generation

The present interest in the "length of a Bible generation" is prompted by the Words of Jesus in the book of Matthew:

> *Matthew 24:34: "Verily I say unto you, This **generation** shall not pass, till all these things be fulfilled."*

Bible students have been fascinated with discovering the meaning of this generation and its length of time as it relates to prophecy.

> *Matthew 24:3: And as he sat upon the mount of Olives, the disciples came unto him privately saying, Tell us, when shall these things be? **And what shall be the sign of thy coming, and of the end of the world?***

The disciples wanted to know:

1.) ...when these things shall be (the Temple destroyed)...

2.) ...what shall be the sign of thy coming (The Second Coming) and of the end of the world (age).

Actually, counting from the time of Jesus' death, *Herod's Temple* would be destroyed within about 40 years (70 AD) by General Titus (later, Emperor Titus) of the Roman army. We know that the Temple was destroyed so obviously a future *Jewish Temple* will be built in Jerusalem that will be polluted by antichrist. Scriptures say that the antichrist personage (*Satan incarnate - Genesis 3:15*) will enter the Jewish Temple during the

Tribulation Period and declare that he is God. This Temple, defiled by the antichrist person, will also be destroyed at the End of the Age.

The End of the Age.

Jesus proceeded to tell the disciples of many things that will occur - (Matthew 24:5-30):

➢ Many shall come in my name saying, I am Christ, and shall deceive many

➢ False prophets deceiving many by showing great signs and wonders

➢ Wars and rumors of war

➢ Famines

➢ Pestilences

➢ Earthquakes

➢ Iniquity abounding

➢ Abomination of desolation

➢ This Gospel of the Kingdom shall be preached in all the world

➢ **Great Tribulation**

➢ The sun be darkened, and the moon shall not give her light, and the stars shall fall from heaven, and the powers of the heavens shall be shaken: then shall appear **the sign of the Son of man – "The Second Advent of Christ."**

Both Bible students and scholars alike ponder

1.) Who is this **generation?**

Answer: Primarily Jews of Daniel's 70th Week of Prophecy but Gentiles as well

2.) When is this **generation?**

Answer: Near the end of the world (age). *Undoubtedly* less than a hundred years since Israel was restored as a nation on May 14, 1948.

3.) How long is a **generation?**

Answer: "See the probabilities following:

The Length of a Bible Generation?

Is the length of a generation **20, 25, 28, 30, 33, 35, 40, 46, 50, 70, 100, 120 years...**or even some other number of years?

The Greek word for generation is "genea," and it is used as meaning that of a particular age or generation. A similar word "genos" sometimes means "stock" or "kind," but never genea. "Length of time" is impertinent to this generation except in relation to the historical time of occurrences. The emphasis on this generation is not to "the length of a generation" **but "to that generation which sees these things begin to come to pass" or see all these things fulfilled.** To that generation, Jesus says,

"Lift up your heads for your redemption draweth nigh" (Luke 21:28).

Generation speculation of Abrahamic Covenant:

Genesis 15:13-16: And he said unto Abram, Know of a surety that thy seed shall be a stranger in a land that is not their's, and shall serve them (Egypt); and they (Egypt) shall afflict them (Israel) **four hundred years***; And also that nation, whom they shall serve, will I judge: and afterward shall they (Israel) come out with great substance (The Exodus). And thou shalt go to thy fathers in peace; thou shalt be buried in a good old age. But* **in the fourth generation** *they shall come hither again: for the iniquity of the Amorites is not yet full.*

We see that this period of Israel in Egypt was four hundred years in length and logically the four hundred years appears to be divided into four periods of one-hundred years each as indicated by the term, "in the fourth generation" of Genesis 15:16.

*(**NOTE:** Of course, Israel was actually in Egypt four hundred and thirty years (Exodus 12:40). It was about thirty years before a Pharaoh came to power that knew not Joseph and slavery began. Joseph was in Egypt years before his father and brethren arrived.)*

In the book of Matthew, we are told that that this generation (*the fig tree nation of Jews*) shall not pass away, **till all these things** (*the tribulation of those days and the coming of the Son of man*) **be fulfilled** (*Matthew 24:32*). Now if Israel is "as a fig tree" when his branch is yet tender, and putteth forth leaves (*a young nation of latter times having been restored on May 14, 1948*), then we should expect the predictions of Jesus to occur **before** May 14, 2048, being a fourth generation (*Genesis 15:16*) of four hundred years. Why before the end of the fourth generation? Because Matthew 24:34 says "Verily I say unto you, This generation (*fourth generation; of 100 years – Genesis 15:16)* shall not pass, **till all these things** (*predictions of Jesus*) **be fulfilled**" - (*Matthew 23:34*). This obviously infers that the climax will occur **before the fourth generation ends**. By adding 100 years to the rebirth of the nation of Israel in May 14, 1948, we obtain the year 2048 (without deducting brief periods of time such as the 75 days between the end of The Great Tribulation and the beginning of the 1000-year Millennial Kingdom of Christ). If we subtract the seven years of The Tribulation from 2048, we have the year 2041 (or earlier). This would conclude that the First Resurrection (translation; rapture) of the church would occur sometimes between 2009 and 2041 or sooner. The writer is not "setting a date," but we are not ignorant of the times and the seasons (I Thessalonians 5:1-5). A spread of about thirty years can hardly be construed to be setting a date.

Jesus derided the unbelieving Pharisees, *"...tempting desired him that he would shew them a sign from heaven."* Jesus reminded them of their ability to predict the weather and yet were unable to discern the signs of the times. The sign of Jonas was the only sign that Jesus gave them (*Matthew 16:1-4*).

Again, **if** this generation of Matthew 24:34 is 100 years in length and this is correct reasoning, we might expect Christ's Second Advent (not the Fist Resurrection; rapture of the church) to occur somewhere between 2009 and 2048. Realizing that the translation (or rapture) of the church (*I Thessalonians 4:13-18; I Corinthians 15:51-58; Revelation 3:10; Titus 2:13; Daniel 9:24-27*) is to occur at least 7 years before The Second Advent of Christ, again we should expect the translation of the church anywhere between the years 2009 to 2041 or sooner.

> *Matthew 24:33: So likewise ye, when ye shall see all these things (Matthew 24), know that it is near (Matthew 24:33), even at the doors.*

From Adam to Abraham is about 20 generations or approximately 2,000 years. Dividing 2,000 years by 20, we get **100 years** for a generation.

Again, the writer does not believe that the length of time of a generation is the main interest here, but that of the generation that is living when these events occur.

> *2 Peter 3:8: But beloved, be not ignorant of this one thing, that one day is with the Lord as a thousand years, and a thousand years as one day.*

Present World Condition

The World System is at such a condition that Anti-Christ could take charge tomorrow (*his aides are busy at work*). Former Christian America is now being ruled by a minority of evil leaders who are blind guides leading the blind. When the Lord comes for His own in the air, (I Thessalonians 4:13-18; I Corinthians 15:51-58), the secular worldly churches will carry on as usual and will not even experience an absence of the Holy Spirit Who had not indwelt them and was not even present in their midst. The church has become so "worldly" that the world is absolutely ready to become "churchy." Even the secular world knows that many church-goers are a sham (2 Corinthians 5:17). (Protestant churches are endorsing sodomite ministers).

There are death rattles in the economy and deadly warnings in weather patterns. Radical Muslims are daily beheading, burning, and slaughtering Christians en masse (*especially in the Mid-East*). The world is teetering on the brink of a moral collapse Experts are warning about an economic collapse. Nothing is sin anymore. All forms of sin have been replaced with words of soft-sounding euphemisms (Viz., gambling is called gaming; abortion is called a woman's right to choose to kill the innocent baby; drunkards are called alcoholics; sin addictions are called diseases (diseases used to be caused by germs); sodomites are called homosexuals (or those of an alternate life style); good is called bad and bad is called good; those living together without the benefit of marriage are white-washed by calling them "fiances." God pronounces a WOE upon those that call bad good and good bad (Isaiah 5:20.

Israel is living on the ragged edge surrounded by her enemies who openly swear to destroy her. America, the greatest and most powerful nation that has ever existed upon earth, has an impostor president without legal citizenship and without a legal social security number from CT, a state that he has never lived in. Our Muslim president despises Israel, rejects true Christianity and greatly honors Islam (the bloody 'religion of the sword"). Hussein Obama has recently come out of the closet to endorse sodomite (homosexual) marriage.

The believer's hope is in the First Resurrection (translation; rapture), of being caught up to meet the Lord in the air (I Thessalonians 4:13-18; I Corinthians 15:51-58; Romans 5:9; Titus 2:13; Revelation 3:10; 4:1; I Thessalonians 5:9). Probably, the atmosphere above will be a Hallelujah Boulevard when Jesus receives His Bride. No doubt, there will be a great host of angels of the heavenly entourage accompanying Jesus and His saints. What a reception! Then, "Look up for your redemption draweth nigh" will be literally fulfilled but WOE upon "earth dwellers."

Israel is God's Timepiece for Prophecy

Gentile time is associated with Israel's place in the world. The prophet, Daniel, outlined Seventy Weeks of Prophecy divided into three spaces of Israel's time among the Gentile world. These Seventy Weeks are equal to 490 years (one week equals 7 years).

Daniel 9:24-27: Seventy weeks are determined upon the people and upon thy holy city, to finish the transgression, and to make an end of sins, and to make reconciliation for iniquity, and to bring in everlasting righteousness, and to seal up the vision and prophecy, and to anoint the most holy. Know therefore and understand, that from the going forth of the commandment to restore and to build Jerusalem unto the Messiah the Prince shall be seven weeks, and threescore and two weeks: the street shall be built again, and the wall, even in troublous times. And after threescore and two weeks shall Messiah be cut off, but not for himself: and the people of the prince that shall come shall destroy the city and the sanctuary; and the end thereof shall be with a flood, and unto the end of the war desolations are determined. And he shall confirm the covenant with many for one week: and in the midst of the week he shall cause the sacrifice and the oblations to cease, and for the overspreading of abominations he shall make it desolate, even until the consummation, and that determined shall be poured upon the desolate.

The 70 Weeks (490 years) are divided into three separate periods of Jewish time that do not necessarily run concurrent with each other:

7 Weeks (49 Years): Began about 536 BC (Ezra 1:1-5) and runs to about 487 BC. This was 70 years after the Babylonian

invasion of Israel in 606 BC. Ezra 7:11 and Nehemiah 2:7 apply to "troublesome times."

62 Weeks (434 yeas): Began about 430 BC to about 3 AD (death of Christ supposed).

Seventieth Week (7 years): Begins near the end of the Church Age and ends near the Second Coming of Christ at the end of Daniel's Seventieth Week.

Dennis Helton
200 Home Place Drive
Easley, SC 29640

INDEX OF WORDS AND PHRASES